Teacher Dispositions

Envisioning Their Role in Education

Kim E. Koeppen
Judith Davison-Jenkins

Rowman & Littlefield Education
Lanham, Maryland • Toronto • Plymouth, UK
2007

Published in the United States of America
by Rowman & Littlefield Education
A Division of Rowman & Littlefield Publishers, Inc.
A wholly owned subsidary of The Rowman & Littlefield Publishing Group, Inc.
4501 Forbes Boulevard, Suite 200, Lanham, Maryland 20706
www.rowmaneducation.com

Estover Road
Plymouth PL6 7PY
United Kingdom

British Library Cataloguing in Publication Information Available

Library of Congress Cataloging-in-Publication Data

Koeppen, Kim E., 1962–
    Teacher dispositions : envisioning their role in education / Kim E.
Koeppen, Judith Davison-Jenkins.
        p. cm.
    Includes bibliographical references.
    ISBN-13: 978-1-57886-582-6 (hardcover : alk. paper)
    ISBN-13: 978-1-57886-583-3 (pbk. : alk. paper)
    ISBN-10: 1-57886-582-4 (hardcover : alk. paper)
    ISBN-10: 1-57886-583-2 (pbk. : alk. paper)
    1. Teachers—United States—Attitudes. 2. Teachers—United States—
Psychology. 3. Teachers—Training of—United States. I. Davison-Jenkins,
Judith, 1945– . II. Title.
    LB1775.2.K64 2007
    370.71'1—dc22   2006101907

Contents

Foreword

There is a schism between those who believe teaching is a profession like law or medicine, requiring a substantial amount of education before one becomes a practitioner, and those who think teaching is a craft like journalism, which is learned principally on the job. (Levine, 2006, pp. 2, 4)

It has always been one of my central beliefs that teaching is challenging intellectual work. Whenever I say that to people, most give me a strange look. Virtually everyone has an opinion about teachers and schools. Schools are so familiar to us that we find it difficult to look at the processes of schooling and teaching analytically. Like the physicist who suggested that fish don't "see" the water in which they exist, most of us fail to really "see" schools because we are so familiar with them—we "swim" in this water without really thinking about it. Over 30 years ago, Seymour Sarason (1972) suggested, in his ethnography on schooling, that we need to make the familiar "strange" again, to really examine it. His suggestion was that we pretend we are from another planet and try to look at schooling with completely new eyes. Although they don't go this far, teacher educators Kim E. Koeppen and Judith Davison-Jenkins in *Teacher Dispositions: Envisioning Their Role in Education* have attempted to "see" through a new lens the dispositions that teachers need to become truly effective and influential educators.

By dispositions, the authors mean the values, commitments, and professional ethics that can help transform a good teacher into a great teacher.

What do I mean when I say that teaching is challenging intellectual work? And what does that have to do with dispositions? I have been an educator—a teacher—for over a quarter of a century. During that entire time, first as a K–12 teacher and then as a teacher educator, I can honestly say I have never been bored. There has always been something new to learn, often about my professional work and content knowledge, but also frequently about the particular idiosyncrasies of the students with whom I worked *intensely*. What else can you call it but intense when an elementary teacher interacts for 6 or 7 hours every day in one room with the same 20–35 small individuals—or when a middle school teacher must meet the needs of perhaps 90–110 early adolescent students each day—or when a high school teacher works with 120–150 young adults per day? Striving to effectively address students' strengths and meet their needs provides a continuous stimulus for teachers to solve problems and make decisions.

At the heart of problem solving lies something called professional judgment. As the opening quote from Arthur Levine (2006) indicates, teachers' professional judgment is at risk more than ever before. And we know that judgment is a stunning combination of reason and emotion. In *Descartes' Error*, Antonio Damasio (1994) makes a compelling scientific argument that there is no judgment without both reason and emotion, thereby asserting the error of Descartes' statement "I think, therefore I am." Through an examination of brain damage in individuals, and making use of the latest in neurological science, Damasio confirms the impressive linkage between what a person feels and what a person thinks—and how both are essential in leading to the individual's judgment.

In the Western world, we are fond of trying to separate reason and emotion, thinking and affect. Fortunately, even influential teachers have not been successful at preserving this dichotomy. Influential teachers have many excellent qualities—they know their content and they know their pedagogy (Ruddell, 1995). But there are also affective and interpersonal components that are necessary to excellent teaching. Most people can recall about three influential teachers—and they can usually say why those teachers were influential. In addition to being knowledgeable and being able to communicate that knowledge, those influential teachers also had "something" else—some quality of caring (Noddings, 1995), of social context (Peterson, Wilkinson, & Hallinan, 1984), and of "community" (DuFour & Eaker, 1998)—that made a difference between a learning experience that was adequate and one that was unforgettable.

There is another term for that really meaningful learning experience—"flow" (Csikszentmihalyi, 1990). Flow is a well-documented state of engagement when the world seems to go away as the individual becomes involved with the task or the idea. Although flow is usually couched as an individual experience, over the years various student groups (from first-graders to doctoral students) and I have experienced "flow" in widely disparate classroom settings when we were engaged in learning together. This was characterized by a state of unity of thought that was almost Zen-like. There is no doubt in my mind that those experiences gave rise to *emotions* that were exhilarating and unforgettable. It is one of the compelling reasons that I teach, and Koeppen and Davison-Jenkins surely reveal the presence of flow in the dispositions that they identify through their research and their students' journals.

Lately, in our efforts to be terribly scientific about education, we have stopped talking a great deal about the affective side of teaching. The accountability movement in education, for example, puts much more emphasis on test scores than on creativity and happiness. Teachers and teacher education programs are to be judged on their outcomes, that is, how much content students learn from their teachers. The affective domain is real, nevertheless, and Koeppen and Davison-Jenkins are attempting to start a conversation among teacher educators about those "often intangible attributes that affect teaching and learning" (p. 1). They bravely take on such soft and squishy terms as "context" and "personal attributes" and "transformations," and they *study* them. In the "knowledge, skills, and dispositions" required of successful teachers, it is easier to focus on knowledge and skills that are easily definable and concrete quantitative variables. Instead, the authors focus on the dispositions, ill-defined constructs that we—teacher educators—know are important, but can't quite get our scholarly heads around. Koeppen and Davison-Jenkins remind us that we need to address these essential components of teaching in a way that is productive for our profession, for all the teacher candidates we educate, and, ultimately, for the K–12 students we serve. The story of their research is both an interesting and important starting point for this conversation.

In this book, Koeppen and Davison-Jenkins introduce a tool (the *personal qualitative inventory*, or PQI, of dispositions) that I hope my colleagues in teacher education will use. Through the PQI, a qualitative tool and journal, the authors have created a beginning rubric for teacher dispositions, a useful instrument for our work in persuading our students to make the familiar strange and to think in a new way about teaching. In addition, the PQI and the discussions among teacher candidates clearly illustrate the transformation that must occur in undergraduate students. They must "grow up" and learn as professionals rather than as "students." They must grow a "teacher identity" that acknowledges a new role—that of legitimate authority—and learn to embrace and celebrate the complexity that is teaching.

I enjoyed reading the journals of students who learned about the subtleties of interpersonal relationships—students who learned the difference between route knowledge and map knowledge (Caine & Caine, 1991). I view map knowledge as what we teach in our preparation programs—how to do guided reading, for example. Route knowledge is actual navigation in the classroom with K–12 students, teaching them, in turn, the map knowledge they will need to achieve familiarity with new content or skills. Map knowledge has always signified theory to me, while route knowledge signifies practice—the application and automaticity of sure mastery of some learning domain.

Finally, I think readers will celebrate that the cooperating teacher finds a place in the pages of our scholarship, even if the cynicism of watching the educational pendulum swing to and fro is revealed. I have to believe that it is the bureaucratic structure of schooling that gives rise to the insular traditionalism that many experienced teachers express as a "lack of time" to seek new knowledge and new ways of doing things. I am struck by the authors' analysis that this stance may be more a function of "a need to maintain some autonomy and/or a need to maintain some professional control over curriculum and instructional strategies" (p. 88).

Teaching is more than simply giving information. To stand and deliver, no matter how charismatically it is done, is not what Koeppen and Davison-Jenkins hope our teacher candidates will focus on in their professional careers. The authors quote Palmer (1998), who states, "depth is depth." Ways of learning our profession—not our "craft"—more deeply are clearly modeled in the pages of this book. I concur with them that we cannot understand the depth of others until we understand our own depth. With this book, the authors have made an important first step in this essential and recursive conversation.

Dana L. Grisham, Ph.D., Multiple Subjects Coordinator
California State University—East Bay

Preface

We wrote this book as a resource for our colleagues in teacher education. Teacher educators, like their counterparts in the K–12 context, take more than their fair share of criticism. Those in government and popular media often see what they do as obsolete or, worse yet, irrelevant. The introduction of standards by the National Council for the Accreditation of Teacher Educators (NCATE) is just one example of measures being taken to ensure quality in teacher education. However, their efforts often feel imposed from on high.

We want to share with our teacher education colleagues our experiences working with the NCATE standards, specifically those associated with teacher dispositions. We want to share those moments when we felt joy and revelation, dynamic movement, hopefulness, and all the other emotions that go along with participating in a huge project. We also want to share those moments of decision making and stepping back and revisiting, as well as disappointment, challenges, and struggles.

How you use our experiences is up to you. You might want to adopt, adapt, or disregard everything that we chronicle. However, in order to do any of these three things, you need to consider what dispositions are and the role you think they should play in the education of teacher candidates—both within your program and in teacher education in general. That is what we want to do: foster dialogue. At no point do we want to give you the impression that we have arrived!

In chapter 1, we situate teacher dispositions within the larger educational picture. We also talk about the role of context and explain how we define dispositions within our specific teacher education program. In chapter 2 we outline the evolution of the instruments we use to assess teacher dispositions, along with the processes involved. In chapters 3 and 4 we focus on how teacher dispositions manifest themselves in our teacher candidates, from their own perspectives. In chapter 5 cooperating teachers weigh in with their perspectives of teacher dispositions in general, as well as those we specifically promote within our courses. Teacher candidates' and cooperating teachers' voices seem to be underrepresented in the dialogue on teacher dispositions. Finally, in chapter 6 we reflect on our journey with teacher dispositions, on what was done as well as what remains undone. Casting a shadow over it all is the overarching question: Can we or should we assess teacher dispositions?

Chapter One

What Are We Looking For?

Once upon a time, two teacher educators who loved their jobs brainstormed ideas for assignments that would both challenge and excite their teacher candidates. They worked diligently to help teacher candidates recognize and appreciate the intricacies of teaching and learning. They also maintained ongoing conversations regarding the larger complexities of schooling and decisions that affect—overtly or covertly—the education of the nation's children. One such conversation focused on policies and processes designed to homogenize the education profession.

These teacher educators worked in an accredited teacher education program, so they agreed to work within certain standard guidelines. Agreeing to these guidelines did not eradicate their concerns about the same. Of particular concern was how best to provide evidence of their teacher candidates' dispositions (one of the guidelines) to the powers that be.

During their initial conversations, they vacillated between belligerence, intrigue, and concern that the people most vested in the educational process (teachers) were not included in the policy-making process. They wanted to stand firm against external, top–down pressure. At the same time, they were attracted to the often intangible attributes that affect teaching and learning. They wanted to help teacher candidates recognize and reflect on the manifestation of their own personal attributes in the public classroom arena. In the end, they followed the raucous road of intrigue. What would you choose?

A BIGGER PICTURE

Acknowledging that the educational process is a complex endeavor is a fairly recent phenomenon. Initially, learning was one-dimensional, whereby the teacher dispensed content and the learner sat quietly and absorbed that content. In the early 20th century, Dewey (1933) challenged this approach by putting forth the notion that the type of interaction between teacher and students, as well as among students, plays a leading role in determining whether and how well students learn. That is, the strategies used to engage students with the content make a difference in learning. Many teacher educators then emphasized both content and pedagogy in their programs.

More recently, educators have recognized the relevance of teachers' personal attributes and the role they play in deciding how content is chosen, delivered, and received (Collinson, 1996; Goodlad, 1990, 1994; Yost, 1997). As teacher educators begin to address personal attributes, focusing on "how a person sees, acts, and lives (teaching by modeling), one could argue that the development of dispositions and ethics is very important in teacher education. It is, however, such a neglected part of teacher education as to be almost nonexistent" (Collinson, 1996, p. 9). The National Network for Educational Renewal (Goodlad, 1994), the Holmes Group (1995), and the National Council for the Accreditation of Teacher Educators or NCATE (2000), among others, are working to remedy this situation at a national level.

We, in turn, address the situation regarding dispositions at a local level within our unique context. In this chapter, we establish the framework for our work by sharing how we came to define teacher dispositions and the role context played in the process.

NCATE (2000) presents dispositions as the values, commitments, and professional ethics that influence behaviors toward students, families, colleagues, and communities, as well as those that affect student learning, motivation, development, and the educators' own professional growth. Because we work within an NCATE-accredited institution, we delved into their documents looking for guidance regarding "how to make these dispositions real and demonstrable to preservice teachers" (Powers, 1999, p. 3). Closer examination supported Maylone's (2002) assertion that NCATE gives teacher educators, teacher candidates, and inservice teachers little information as to what constitutes positive or effective teacher dispositions. Still others (Balzano & Murray, 2003; Taylor & Wasicsko, 2000; Wenzlaff, 1998) are concerned that the research literature on teacher dispositions provides little assistance with definitions.

Dispositions seem to be more intangible than other aspects of teaching, such as content and pedagogy. As Usher (2002) explains,

> Dispositions are determiners of behavior though not in a one-to-one way. They are constellations of personal meanings from which behaviors spring and thus they do determine the probability of effectiveness for one's professional choices and behaviors. As such, dispositions are not open to direct measurement, however, dispositions can be inferred and inferences can be subjected to standards of validity and reliability for use in research and other measurement tasks. (pp. 1–2)

The nebulous nature of teacher dispositions seems to stifle people's desire to formally work with them. While the task seems daunting, "it is important for teacher educators to know and understand the dispositions of effective teachers, so as to design experiences that will help to develop these characteristics in students and to help students discover if they have the 'dispositions to teach'" (Taylor & Wasicsko, 2000, p. 2).

We believe that teacher educators can help their teacher candidates to recognize their existing dispositions, to discover dispositions that might be missing, and to cultivate new ones. Teacher educators can foster this examination and growth by developing assessment processes and instruments to use for both external and self-assessment. To this end, we embarked on a whirlwind journey to clarify teacher dispositions and then apply them within the context of our teacher education program.

We recognize the interconnectedness between teacher dispositions and effective teachers (see, e.g., Demmon-Berger, 1986; Good & Brophy, 1994; Leithwood, 1990; Noddings, 1992) and teacher identity (see, e.g., Banner & Cannon, 1997; Danielewicz, 2001; Kottler & Zehm, 2000; Palmer, 1998). Research on effective teachers and teacher identity is ever so important to enhancing teaching and learning as well as promoting the growth of education as a profession. However, we intend to present a tightly focused account of our work with teacher dispositions. Our intention is not to present our work as a static final product, but as a vibrant, flexible process that expands and changes as we continue to examine teacher dispositions critically and their use with our teacher candidates.

CLARIFYING OUR VIEW OF DISPOSITIONS

We believe that for the development and implementation of assessment instruments surrounding teacher dispositions to be successful, you must take into consideration the context in which they will be addressed. Context is superimposed on every aspect of the decision-making and implementation processes; context determines the depth and breadth to addressing teacher dispositions (as well as other issues and concepts) over the course of an entire program. Acknowledging and working within your context will enable you to better connect the practical and the theoretical within your specific teacher education program.

In the remainder of this chapter, you will gain insights into the context within which we work and the definitions of teacher dispositions that emerged within that context. Figure 1 provides an overview of our endeavors to clarify our views of dispositions. We were spurred to action by NCATE standards. While we believe strongly that you may choose to start at any point and/or to proceed in any order, we do believe that working through and struggling with each phase will strengthen your ownership of the assessment processes and instruments you develop.

As teacher educators in an NCATE-accredited institution, we are obliged on some level to provide evidence of how our programs assess teacher candidates' knowledge, skills, and dispositions. Knowledge and skills tend to be quite tangible and means of assessment are readily available (e.g., course grades and standardized tests). As mentioned earlier, dispositions are much less tangible and no means of assessment was available within our program.

We moved from our examination of the NCATE (2000) standards and the bigger picture of teacher dispositions to a review of the Interstate New Teacher Assessment and Support Consortium (INTASC) standards (1992), the Minnesota Board of Teaching (BOT) standards (2000), and our own College of Education conceptual framework. To

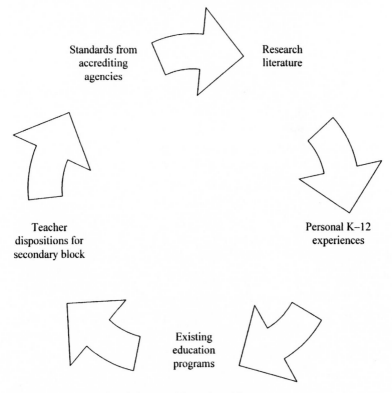

Standards from accrediting agencies

Research literature

Teacher dispositions for secondary block

Personal K–12 experiences

Existing education programs

Figure 1.   Process of Defining Teaching Dispositions

this end, we were able to see if any portion of these documents addressed expectancies regarding dispositions. Like NCATE (2000), INTASC (1992), and BOT (2000) standards, our conceptual framework provided no readily adaptable information to further our development of assessment processes or instruments for teacher dispositions.

We did find commonalities in language, such as standards and substandards that resembled the definition of dispositions provided by NCATE (2000). This seemed to imply that dispositions were a part of the foundation of our existing program. We then waded through the language of these documents to develop specific categories that would lend themselves to assessment procedures. The willingness to suspend judgment, the ability to exhibit respect for self and others, and the inclination to respond maturely to situations are examples of dispositions that cut across these foundational documents.

The limited studies focusing on dispositions draw heavily from research on the characteristics of effective teachers. In fact, our early conversations about the characteristics of successful teachers' dispositions were informed by effective teacher research as well as the literature on teacher identity. Researchers such as Palmer (1998) and Banner and Cannon (1997) talk about the human ingredients that are a part of our makeup, which then manifest themselves in our classroom practices. This focus coincides with the current shift away from a primary emphasis on content and pedagogical knowledge toward including the inter- and intrapersonal knowledge and skills of effective teachers (Collinson, 1996).

Inter- and intrapersonal knowledge and skills are attributes that should permeate all aspects of the teaching profession. Although they are often innate, these qualities can be learned or developed if you can identify them in yourself and then consciously work to bring them into your persona as a teacher. However, containing dispositions with a single definition seems limiting since their manifestation is boundless. This is because of the unique ways that dispositions emerge from the whole person.

As we contemplated how we would use the complex concept of teacher dispositions with our teacher candidates, we wanted the information presented in educational theory to resonate within educational practice. This connection would provide the grounding in reality necessary to strengthen our trust in the characteristics we identified as being trustworthy and believable. To accomplish this, we examined each dispositional category that we culled from the literature in light of our varied experiences in multiple positions with K–12 public school settings.

We kept the categories that matched with what we witnessed in our school experiences in an effort to increase the chances that the dispositions would be recognizable to our teacher candidates. The following ten categories seemed to best describe teacher dispositions at this initial stage of our development: (1) actively engaging in small/large class settings, (2) thoughtful and responsive listening, (3) cooperating/collaborating, (4) respecting self and others, (5) actively engaging in reflection, (6) being prepared, (7) continuously learning, (8) responding to situations, (9) responding to feedback, and (10) attending class.

We simultaneously investigated the history of contemplation that existed in our college of education prior to NCATE (2000) expectancies regarding dispositions. We examined expectancies as outlined by the education faculty for two field experiences and student teaching. We looked specifically for characteristics associated with teacher dispositions. What we discovered were numerous implications, but again, no explicit references to the concept of teacher dispositions or how they might manifest themselves within our teacher education program.

We work in a secondary education licensure program at a large state university. The lack of systematic attention to teacher dispositions from a program perspective contributes to the elusiveness of the concept for our teacher candidates. Kim teaches an educational foundations course and Judy teaches a curriculum course; these classes are taken concurrently with an extended field experience to form what is known as a Secondary Block. As a result of this Secondary Block, we both work with the same set of students each semester.

While there is no rigid scope and sequence, teacher candidates do take an introduction to education course at the start of the secondary program and take the Secondary Block the semester prior to their student teaching experience. The concept of teacher dispositions is introduced in the initial education course, where teacher candidates begin a cursory examination of their own attitudes; however, there is no assessment process or instrument in place at the program level.

In our Secondary Block, we stress the importance teacher dispositions play in the triad of their evolving teacher identity, that is, knowledge, skills, and dispositions that will accompany them into their future classrooms. Our intent is not only to help teacher candidates develop a depth of understanding regarding teacher dispositions, but also to identify their own dispositions and to develop a sense of the symbiotic relationship dispositions have with knowledge and skills. We also try to alert individuals to any dispositions that might negatively affect future teaching and learning contexts in the hope that we can address them together.

Our goal was to weave all the information and insights we accumulated into a procedure that would complement existing assessments while explicitly focusing on characteristics of teacher dispositions.

LOOKING AHEAD

Throughout this book, we hope to provide you an up-close and personal view of our work with teacher dispositions. We outline the ways in which we worked with teacher dispositions, our teacher candidates' perceptions of this work, and our reflections on it all in chapter 2. Chapters 3 and 4 contain a plethora of teacher candidates' voices as they worked with dispositions initially in our Secondary Block courses and then in their K–12 field placements.

We explore cooperating teachers' perceptions of dispositions in chapter 5. These multiple perspectives on teacher dispositions reinforce the complex nature of this aspect of teacher education. Our parting words are an attempt to make sense of where and how dispositions fit with their more-established counterparts—knowledge and skills—and to raise questions that will encourage more and possibly different conversations concerning teacher education.

Chapter Two

How Do We Work with What We See?

It was the first day of class, and the professors walked into their respective classrooms with some new anxieties accompanying the usual butterflies of anticipation. Even though the well was deep, filled with years of experience and buoyed from recent collaboration with a trusted colleague, the inevitable anxiety and vulnerability that is felt by an educator was present. This was a different context than previous semesters. Not only were new faces occupying the seats in the room, but the professors were also embarking on a novel venture—the introduction and assessment of "teacher dispositions" to their course repertoires.

The lesson plans were meticulously prepared to prime the teacher candidates for their first experience with the concept and its application to their budding careers. The professors invoked team teaching strategies to build upon one another's comments as they addressed these new faces. In addition, numerous clichés ran through their minds: We're jumping in with both feet. It's time to practice what you preach. This is where the rubber meets the road.

Still, the questions lingered. How would the teacher candidates respond? Would the professors successfully field the questions and address the emotions that would surely arise? What adjustments would have to be made by the professors to encourage teacher candidates' engagement with this concept as an integral aspect of their teacher identity? Could the professors create the necessary balance and integration as dispositions joined knowledge and skills in the teacher education program?

Most teacher educators hope that their courses will influence teacher candidates' beliefs and attitudes. Although some research indicates that information from teacher education courses loses significance or is mitigated once these candidates enter the classroom as student teachers (Deal & Chatman, 1989; Koeppen, 1996; Lortie, 1975; Ross, 1988), other studies suggest that associations with particular teacher education faculty (Su, 1992) and courses (Fehn & Koeppen, 1998; Goodman, 1986; Goodman & Fish, 1997; Ross, 1988; Su, 1992) can influence student teachers' knowledge of and commitment to particular instructional strategies.

We lean toward the optimistic, tending to believe that if teacher education can influence pedagogy, it might also influence dispositions. As a result, we designed an instrument (rubric) and a process to assess teacher dispositions. We were, in turn, interested in examining our teacher candidates' cognitive and affective experiences with assessing teacher dispositions. To accomplish this, we engaged in reflective inquiry (Valli, 1992, 1997) during the recursive design, implementation, redesign, and reimplementation stages in our respective courses. During and after each semester in which we taught our courses, we worked to live up to Valli's (1997) notion of reflective thinkers, that is, people who "are critical of the ideas that occur to them . . . [weighing] competing claims in their search for evidence, which will help them resolve their doubts and perplexity" (p. 68).

Specifically, we engaged in "deliberative reflection" as well as "personalistic reflection" (Valli, 1992, 1997). Deliberative reflection focuses on a wide range of teaching concerns, and decisions are "based on a variety of sources: research, experience, the advice of other teachers, personal beliefs and values, and so forth. No one voice dominates" (1992, p. 77). Personalistic reflection asks teachers to focus on "understanding the reality of their students in order to give them the best care possible," thus increasing their "ability to empathize" (p. 78). Our attempts to understand better the reality of our teacher candidates' experiences helps us to support their efforts to comprehend the role of teacher dispositions within their larger teacher identity (Banner & Cannon, 1997; Palmer, 1998). This reflective process also enhances our teacher identities as we explore, grow, and learn more about teacher dispositions.

In the remainder of this chapter, we share our journey, taking you through the trials and tribulations associated with our ever-evolving assessment processes and instruments. And since they have a profound influence on our thinking, we include our teacher candidates' perceptions of both the assessment processes and instruments. We have come to think of this journey as a rollercoaster ride; we hope that the thrill and excitement of our ride encompasses you. We also encourage you to think about how you might respond to similar views provided from the peaks and valleys of your own rollercoaster.

OUR INITIAL VIEW OF ASSESSMENT

Instrument

In the beginning, we chose to create a rubric that contained the categories and descriptors that we believed embodied the essence of what we found during the process of clarifying the characteristics of teacher dispositions (outlined in chapter 1). We did this because we tend to agree with Albee and Piveral (2003) that "the complex and affective dimensions of dispositions [must be] organized into an instrument" to allow teacher candidates to identify and monitor "their effective dispositions as well as to provide a process to improve areas of concern" (p. 349). Creating the actual rubric was made easier in part because of the time we devoted to developing explicit definitions of teacher dispositions as well as a strong rationale for their place in reflective teacher education (LaBoskey, 1994).

As you will recall from chapter 1, the specific categories of dispositions we devised included (1) actively engaging in small and large class settings, (2) thoughtful and responsive listening, (3) cooperating and collaborating, (4) respecting self and others, (5) actively engaging in reflection, (6) being prepared, (7) continuously learning, (8) responding to situations, (9) responding to feedback, and (10) attendance.

Once these categories were in place, we labored over the language needed to describe accurately and clearly what the often abstract characteristics of teacher dispositions might look like—how we and the teacher candidates might recognize them within the context of the university classroom. The language of Interstate New Teacher Assessment and Support Consortium (INTASC, 1992) was helpful in the development of specific descriptors for the aforementioned categories. In the end, the categories with their descriptors seemed to naturally cluster into *interactions with others* and *professionalism*. Thus, we divided our rubric into these two larger sections.

Finally, we determined how to quantify students' progress on each disposition using qualitative language. *Consistently*, *usually*, *occasionally*, and *rarely* were the descriptors we chose to delineate varying degrees of accomplishment with respect to each of the dispositions represented in the rubric. In an effort to promote the assessment of teacher dispositions as a developmental process, we decided to give a midterm grade-in-progress, and to record only the score from the end of the semester. This allowed for an entire semester's worth of feedback, reflection, and growth. (See appendix 1 for the original rubric.)

Processes

Academic freedom allows for differentiation among professors teaching the same course. Although we kept our colleagues informed about our endeavors with teacher dispositions, we did not push for universal use across the program. Consequently, the assessment instruments and processes described herein were used only with those teacher candidates taking our Secondary Block courses. We faced some additional challenges as a result of this.

Students at every level talk to one another; consequently, "Why don't students in the other Secondary Block have to do this?" was a common question. This question actually provided a nice springboard for discussions about the right to academic freedom, which our teacher candidates could relate directly to their future classrooms. We also directed their attention toward expanding responsibilities regarding the knowledge, skills, and dispositions they were to display and build on as professionals.

Furthermore, in order to help teacher candidates connect teacher dispositions to a broader educational context, we included a narrative paragraph in each of our course syllabi. This paragraph gave an overview of the role of dispositions in effective teaching and NCATE's (2000) emphasis on assessing these dispositions among teacher candidates:

> Promoting dispositions requisite of those in the teaching profession are increasingly being recognized as a fundamental responsibility of teacher education (please refer to the NCATE and INTASC websites linked to the College of Education homepage). As a result, Drs. Jenkins and Koeppen are creating a rubric whereby professors can guide teacher candidates' development of dispositions that research deems beneficial to promoting growth and learning in others. Diligent note-taking will enable me to monitor your progress throughout the semester.
>
> You will receive a formal update on your progress prior to going into the classroom for your field experience and then a final assessment at the end of the semester. If you are scoring in the C-D range in a variety of areas and/or are frequently in that range in limited areas, I will contact you quickly so that we can clear up any misunderstandings as to expectations.

The dispositions rubric itself was then distributed.

In the first semester of implementation, we tried to maximize our conversations with our teacher candidates by addressing the process and rubric as well as the concept of teacher dispositions itself in different ways on different days. Kim used class time to talk with students about the processes surrounding the dispositions rubric. She emphasized that this was intended as a reflective tool, a means for determining whether their self-perceptions and how others view them were aligned (Palmer, 1998), in other words, "Do you see what I see?" She explained that at midterm, they would conduct a self-assessment by marking the dispositions rubric according to their perspectives. They would submit their rubrics and receive professor assessment based on the professor's perspectives to date.

The insights provided by both the teacher candidate and the professor marking the same dispositions rubric would then provide the opportunity for conversation and potential growth. Kim explained that their dispositions would be assessed again at the end of the semester using the same process. This final assessment would be added to their summative course grade. The process and rubric would be the same for each course of our Secondary Block; the context in which it all took place was the only thing that changed.

On a subsequent day, Judy put our teacher candidates into small groups and asked them to critique the dispositions rubric. She invited open-ended written comments about the rubric, samples of which were then explored in class in an effort to heighten their ownership of and, therefore, comfort with the dispositions rubric as well as the assessment process. Since we viewed the dispositions rubric as a dynamic instrument, we wanted to obtain information from our teacher candidates—the immediate stakeholders—that would inform the subsequent revision process. To this end, we collected the groups' written comments to examine in more depth.

Throughout the ensuing weeks, we each monitored and documented the occurrence of dispositions in our respective courses. This process resembled ethnographic field notes in that we took notes throughout class (e.g., during large- and small-group discussions), and expanded on those notes after class. Our notes provided the foundation for feedback to individual teacher candidates as well as our own critical reflection. We followed through with the midterm assessment process in each course and held individual conversations where necessary to help clarify perspectives, language, and expectations. We also took advantage of such opportunities to provide concrete suggestions for personal reflection and growth over the second portion of the semester.

In an effort to help our teacher candidates better understand multiple perspectives, we tried to focus their reflections on those dispositions where there was a disconnect between what they recorded and what we recorded. We encouraged them to think more deeply about how and why these differences occurred. In addition, they were encouraged to think about any changes that they might need to make in order to better ensure that the teacher identity they intend others to see shines through brightly. We followed the same process at the end of the semester and included this score in their summative grade for each course.

Reflections

In the beginning, we were given a pseudo-directive—incorporate assessment for dispositions into the secondary teacher education program—and our reflections focused on how best to fulfill it. However, we had experienced the resentment associated with top–down edicts throughout our careers and were determined to have ownership of anything we implemented. As a result, we started our journey knowing that any assessment we created would go through numerous revisions before it was "done."

Our early conversations helped us define the concept of teacher dispositions and enhanced our initial introduction of the instrument and processes to our teacher candidates. Once we started to implement what we had created, and received concrete feedback and questions from our teacher candidates, our reflective conversations took on a whole new dimension.

Two primary concerns emerged for us during our first month of working with teacher dispositions. First, the physical act of recording observed behaviors seemed staggering. For instance, how frequently should we observe, how could we quantify duration and intensity, and how could we maintain the acute awareness needed in the classroom to note behaviors in selected categories? Second, just as we needed to feel ownership, so too did our teacher candidates. Our initial attempts at cultivating this feeling did not materialize as we had anticipated. We were determined to enhance their ownership of both the instrument and the processes used to assess teacher dispositions.

Fortunately, a previously scheduled presentation of our work with teacher dispositions at a collegewide forum coincided with the emergence of these concerns regarding observations and ownership. We shared these two concerns during our presentation and sought insights from our colleagues.

In general, our dispositions rubric was well received. Our colleagues saw merit in making explicit those dispositions that we often assume are embodied inherently within our teacher candidates. In addition, they appreciated our efforts to bring these complex dispositions to the forefront in concrete ways for specific discussion and analysis.

One colleague asked us a question in response to our concern about teacher candidates' ownership. He asked if there was a way to include more detailed self-assessment, that is, moving teacher candidates beyond simply marking the rubric at the midpoint and end of the course. This question sparked considerable reflection as we thought about changing the rubric for the upcoming semester. We considered how best to give teacher candidates more responsibility and to provide them with the space and time necessary to support self-assessment. None of our colleagues had suggestions to help ease our recording woes.

Superimposed on these reflective considerations were the comments and concerns expressed by our teacher candidates through the written feedback from the initial small groups as well as through individuals' oral comments. It was important to us that teacher candidates have the opportunity to voice their thoughts, questions, and concerns so that we could better develop ways to encourage ownership, alleviate fears, and clarify expectations. The teacher candidates' voices we share in the remainder of this chapter represent those that most directly sparked our revision of the processes and products associated with teacher dispositions. We devote chapters 3 and 4 to an in-depth portrayal of the myriad voices of our teacher candidates and their experiences with and insights from actually exploring their personal teacher dispositions.

One of the strongest initial reactions from our teacher candidates was "Who do you think you are to make judgments about my personal qualities and then grade me on them?" We were not particularly surprised by this reaction. In our early conversations, we wrestled with this issue in a roundabout way. We believe dispositions are a personal by-product of the interactions between our identity and integrity as outlined by Palmer (1998). As such, dispositions are linked directly to who we are. Rokeach (1968) argues, "beliefs that are linked closely to [people's] ego—sense of self—are more important than any others" (p. 4). We anticipated that any attempt to pass judgment within this realm, however well intentioned, would meet with resistance. Therefore, although the question was often posed in a combative tone, the sentiment did merit critical consideration from us.

At this initial stage, we addressed this question through class discussion. We explained that teacher dispositions were indeed grounded in their personal qualities. However, we were focusing on personal qualities that manifest themselves in very public places— the school and classroom contexts. As teacher candidates, they would soon be the vehicles through which curriculum and instruction are conveyed and school climate established and/or reinforced.

In order for these processes to be positive and effective, teacher candidates would need to recognize the role of dispositions in addition to the importance of strong content knowledge and pedagogical skills. Dispositions require people to not only recognize their presence (or absence), but to also consciously act upon (or develop) them in whatever context they present themselves. Our context of concern was that of the school culture and those dispositions most closely intertwined with being a teacher.

Another concern centered upon large class sizes, which they believed made it difficult to participate regularly in whole-class discussions—one of the categories. Some teacher candidates even declared a sense of entitlement for proof from each of us as to how we monitored them in these large-group contexts. Our teacher candidates were not yet comfortable with the concept of teacher dispositions, and they did not trust us to play fair. They also expressed a need to know "what is meant by" the descriptors in some of the categories, for example, obtaining a sample of what reflection looks like.

When we thought about addressing this anxiety, we first thought about the old adage "Actions speak louder than words." In our case, we tried to combine actions with words. That is, we asked our teacher candidates to trust that we were assessing teacher dispositions for developmental rather than punitive purposes. We then promised to engage in metacognition throughout the semester on each of the various dispositions put before them. Hesitantly, they agreed and we charged ahead.

A possible explanation for teacher candidates' apprehension is that we were seeking to make the familiar strange by asking them to think about their chosen profession in new and complex ways. In addition, we may have encountered the preconceived notion that most teacher candidates bring with them to education courses "that they already have what it takes to be a good teacher, and that therefore they have little to learn from the formal study of teaching" (Kennedy, 1997, p. 4). There are times when we believe they are merely seeing the world of teaching through naive eyes, which we hope both maturity and experience will address.

In spite of some apprehensions, teacher candidates did see benefits to using the teacher dispositions rubric. One group commented, "it is a good training tool for learning who we are. It helps us discipline ourselves. We learn about our strengths and weaknesses." Others noted that it helped them to "stay in class in body and mind." Still others alluded to the notion that many of the dispositions could apply to their future students. For example, they wanted their future students to be prepared and actively engaged in the learning experience.

OUR SECOND VIEW OF ASSESSMENT

New Instruments

Buoyed by the comments from our colleagues and our teacher candidates, we made revisions for the upcoming semester. We made minor categorical changes in the teacher dispositions rubric and changes in the language of some of the descriptors (see appendix 2). We also created a narrative outline of the teacher dispositions and allowed space for immediate changes that resulted from teacher candidates' critique (see appendix 3). This outline was a supplement to the rubric.

Even though the content was the same in both the outline and the rubric, the variety of formats seemed to address a wider range of learning styles. Finally, we included a template for them to self-assess, that is, reflect on each disposition on a daily basis and record evidence related to the various dispositions (see appendix 4). We made these changes to address issues of clarity, which we hoped would in turn reduce teacher candidates' anxieties and enhance their appreciation for the role dispositions play in the teaching and learning process. We used these three assessment instruments for the next two semesters.

New Processes

We also changed the process by which we introduced our teacher candidates to the concept of teacher dispositions and the assessment thereof. Rather than waiting to get asked, we started each semester with our response to the question "Who do you think you are . . . ?" (outlined earlier). We were also more systematic at engaging teacher candidates in a critique of the instruments and processes. To this end, we developed the following guiding questions:

- Is there a category that you think should be added to the 10 that are already selected for the rubric?
- Notice the bullet that has no descriptor under each category. What descriptor(s) do you think should be added in each category?
- Language needs to convey, as much as possible, precise messages. Is there any language in the descriptors or in the rubric that needs further definition or clarification?

Teacher candidates thought about these questions individually and shared their ideas in subsequent small groups. We then addressed some of the concerns and comments as a whole group. From the outset, we felt as if we and our teacher candidates would learn about teacher dispositions somewhat simultaneously. We viewed the process as one of trial and error, which was dependent on communication to continuously explore what dispositions are, how to monitor them in ourselves, how to determine growth, and how to measure value.

The changes we made after that first semester allowed us to better convey this sense of shared ownership. We believe the feedback from our teacher candidates became more critical and less combative and antagonistic as a result of the changes we made. Their feedback, as outlined below, continued to fuel our rollercoaster ride with teacher dispositions.

Reflections

Generally, our teacher candidates supported the existing categories of teacher dispositions by indicating that they "covered the basic qualities a teacher should have" and provided an "excellent overview to stimulate their personal thinking." Some were concerned about the language becoming confusing if other categories were added. As one teacher candidate commented,

> I feel that the categories already included cover the major points of professional development in the field; with minor effort, some categories could be extended to encompass any eventualities. By adding more categories, there is also the risk of bureaucracy of a sort. Creating new categories might cause redundancies or confusion.

A few teacher candidates presented the possibility of combining *respect* with *professionalism*, but did not press the issue after a whole-class discussion. A few others suggested adding "flexibility" to the categories in an effort to build on readings from previous education courses. Yet another noted, "according to several readings we have been assigned in our teaching classes, putting the students first is a teacher's number one priority. I believe that in order for a teacher to put the students first, she or he must be flexible."

We actually used these suggestions to cultivate immediate and subsequent class discussions about the complexities and intricacies of teacher dispositions. We talked about how categories can seem to overlap and/or how things that we do in our professional lives may contain elements of a variety of dispositions. While our teacher candidates were fairly comfortable with the categories of dispositions, they did have suggestions or concerns regarding specific descriptors.

The limitations of language become apparent when trying to illuminate the abstract for a large audience of diverse learners. Our teacher candidates seemed to relish the opportunity to offer input that would massage the meanings and/or expand the list of behaviors matched to the dispositional category. The descriptors attempt to create common understanding of each disposition's characteristics. Professors need the descriptors to guide them in the assessment process as they note observable behavior that declares disposition activity. Teacher candidates need clear descriptors so they can monitor themselves and record evidence of disposition activity. Therefore, the guiding question regarding descriptors was a valuable tool for capturing the diversity of perspectives within our groups.

Several teacher candidates wanted *enthusiasm* included at some point in the instruments. Others wanted to include some recognition of the physical attributes they associated with being a thoughtful and responsive listener, for example, "eye contact, body language, and facial expressions that connote attentiveness." There were also issues of clarity, for example, "does suspending judgment mean being open-minded?" The descriptors related to the category *continuous learning* were also elusive for our teacher candidates. They sought more concrete examples of what this disposition might look like in our courses. Some suggested that "taking notes on the important ideas shared by classmates" would be a good indicator of this disposition.

For the most part, the unique concerns of each class were addressed verbally, with all of us making appropriate additions to the narrative outline and corresponding rubric. No permanent changes were made to the rubric during these two semesters. Affording teacher candidates the opportunity to alter the teacher dispositions instruments through deliberate class discussion and encouraging them to reflect on a daily basis seemed to facilitate their ownership.

The increase in shared responsibility on the part of the teacher candidates for assessing their teacher dispositions eliminated many of the observational concerns we had identified and discussed at our collegewide forum the previous semester. Individual conversations were also enhanced now that professors and teacher candidates both had more detailed narratives regarding their perceptions of specific dispositions. Our talking points became much more explicit.

There seems to be no substitute for experience combined with critical reflection. Not only did our assessment instruments improve, but so too did our ability to implement and negotiate the entire process. We became more adept at addressing an audience that might be resistant to formal examination of their teacher dispositions. We better anticipated concerns and were able to dispel many during our initial introductions. At least there appeared to be less confusion or anxiety as evidenced by a substantial decrease in questions, concerns, and/or complaints raised by our teacher candidates.

OUR THIRD VIEW OF ASSESSMENT

Broader Issues

Although we had new and improved instruments and processes, we were far from done. One continuous overarching concern from our teacher candidates was the issue of assigning actual points to teacher dispositions that would then count toward their course grade. Our ongoing reflections included this same issue; however, we had directed our early energies toward the definitional aspects surrounding teacher dispositions. As our teacher candidates grew more comfortable with the concept of teacher dispositions (as we defined them) and the role these play in the teaching and learning context, we felt better equipped to turn our attentions to the nuances of assessment. One question plagued us: Would our teacher candidates value dispositions if they were not graded?

We combed through and discussed two semesters' worth of notes, teacher candidates' comments, and their actual use of the second iteration of our teacher dispositions materials (refer to appendixes 3 and 4). Then we talked and talked and talked. Out of a seemingly random dialogue, a pattern started to emerge. We recognized that portions of our teacher dispositions instruments did appear more tangible than others, and we discovered that the intangible aspects were causing our teacher candidates the most distress.

At this point, we were exhausted. It took a conscious effort to remember our foundational belief in and commitment to maintaining dynamic rather than static instruments and processes. Would we ever be done?

Most Recent Instruments

We quickly decided the answer was "No," and set out to revise our instruments once again; this time we constructed two new types of assessment. We decided to assess the more tangible elements with a rubric that would receive points based on self- and professor-evaluation (a continuation of the previous process). This rubric contained the following: large-group participation, small-group participation, preparedness, and attendance, and we identified it as Class Participation (see appendix 5).

The remaining more intangible elements—listening, cooperation and collaboration, respect, reflection, continuous learning, and professionalism—were kept as the foundation of our teacher dispositions. We decided to use a journal format for this instrument that relied more heavily on self-assessment. We wanted to enable teacher candidates to examine each disposition in light of their personal interactions over the course of the semester. Thus, we asked them to generate a *personal qualitative inventory* (PQI) of their teacher dispositions. This PQI would receive critical feedback from us, but we would not assign evaluative points (see appendix 6).

Most Recent Processes

At first our teacher candidates seemed to value the Class Participation rubric more than the PQI. The PQI was not graded, so why should they put forth any effort to complete it? We were not particularly surprised by this. However, devaluing the PQI was not the only expressed sentiment. Many teacher candidates merely expressed their dislike of journaling for a variety of reasons—they were poor writers, they did not know what to write, they did not know how to think about things deeply, and/or they found it difficult to remember and thus compile an inventory.

Other teacher candidates were not cognizant of what they were doing that might relate to the various elements of teacher dispositions. Still others were simply not used to engaging in this type of thinking process and were uncomfortable with these new demands. Our newest iteration required a bigger sell from us! Were we up to the challenge?

Our latest changes in this entire process evolved from our believing that we now needed to work harder to convince our students of the importance of working with teacher dispositions through the non-graded PQI. Instead of first introducing the notion of teacher dispositions—instruments and process—and then connecting it to teacher candidates' prior knowledge and experiences, we reversed the order.

We now start the process by asking our teacher candidates to share their prior knowledge and experiences surrounding teaching. The resulting list is then loosely categorized by the teacher candidates into knowledge, skills, and dispositions. The questions and musings that emerge during this process provide the necessary springboard to discuss the interconnectedness between the knowledge, skills, dispositions, and the whole person who walks into the classroom. Although this is a time-consuming process, it helps give the role of self-analysis and self-knowledge with respect to teacher dispositions a practical perspective.

Another crucial element to the success of the PQI is the critical feedback we provide to each preservice teacher individually at midterm. Our commitment to creating a written conversation with our teacher candidates around the PQI demonstrates that we honor the process in which they are engaged. Initially, we read the PQIs to gain a sense of what our teacher candidates are inventorying; that is, do they recognize these teacher dispositions within themselves in some way, shape, or form? Next, we determine if our teacher candidates have a sense that they are going somewhere with each disposition—engaging in a personal dialogue around the presence or absence of particular dispositions at various times in an effort to promote personal growth.

During this more in-depth reading, we worked to validate our teacher candidates' endeavors. We provided commentary in the form of questions and/or statements that supported an individual's thoughtfulness or encouraged a closer examination of seemingly generic entries. We were determined that our teacher candidates move away from sheer description of classroom activities toward examination of their experiences and reactions during participation. At times, we acknowledged specific growth as we saw it unfolding, which either confirmed an individual's perception of progress or gave them a different perspective. In addition, the PQI afforded us the opportunity to glean a more complex and well-rounded perspective of our teacher candidates and their evolving teacher identities.

When we returned the PQIs with our feedback, the room became still with a silence we did not want to interrupt. Generally, our teacher candidates were engrossed in reading the comments, and often wrote initial responses to questions and perspectives that promoted the feeling of a private conversation. This process, in turn, seemed to foster a better buy-in from our teacher candidates. For the most part, our teacher candidates seemed to have a better understanding of what they needed to look for in themselves throughout the remainder of the semester. Those who were doing well continued to do so; those who were not seemed to improve, albeit some more than others.

Most Recent Reflections

Our use of the PQI seems to have sparked serious consideration of teacher dispositions and their place in education. Our teacher candidates now appear more engaged in the process of identifying, monitoring, and appreciating teacher dispositions. They recognize the authenticity of the categories and descriptors more readily. They also value the opportunity to self-assess and, once combined with professor feedback, see the chance to engage in a conversation to promote growth in their teacher identity.

The quality of information we amassed, the luxury of time, and hindsight help us realize that we have made several solid and reasonable changes to the instruments and processes by which we assess teacher dispositions. These changes have also sparked more thoughtful feedback from our teacher candidates, which fuels our critical reflection and solidifies our belief that we will never be "done."

Recently, our teacher candidates shared that they feel that they engage in continuous learning every day in class. This is a rather euphoric way of thinking about the daily experience in a classroom. While it may be true, it has credence only if the teacher candidates can actually provide concrete evidence, which takes the statement out of the realm of lofty statements and places it in the reality of what was learned. To this end, teacher candidates suggested additional descriptors such as researching topics discussed in class or texts, and documenting how new knowledge could be applied to future classrooms.

When it comes to cooperation and collaboration, teacher candidates believe that they have had numerous experiences with these two dispositions because they have been involved in group work or what is labeled cooperative learning in many courses. They have the tendency to view cooperation and collaboration as behaviors utilized in small-group settings and, to a lesser degree, in whole-class settings. Their comments emphasized the importance of establishing a safe and encouraging environment for participation, with all ideas receiving due respect.

Teacher candidates were interested in adding language that would explicitly guide their peers to fulfill individual responsibilities associated with cooperation and collaboration. Two additional recommendations were that all teacher candidates take on different group roles rather than adopting a "comfort role" such as leader or writer and not changing, and build on others' ideas, such as linking the ideas produced by the group and asking one another challenging questions. These comments suggest that our teacher candidates were thinking of cooperation and collaboration as dispositions associated closely with small-group work among students. One of our tasks was to help them broaden that perspective, to begin thinking about how this disposition might play out among teachers and other school faculty and staff.

Our teacher candidates indicated that *respect* was another teacher disposition with which they enjoyed a long relationship. Respect can be taken for granted or withheld, using conditional or context-based rationales to justify either reaction. In addition, it is a word that defies universal definition. The abstract, often multidimensional nature of respect required deliberate examination. Hence, our teacher candidates needed to raise their consciousness of the applications, implications, and cause-and-effect patterns of respect in order to suggest additional language for the descriptors or, ultimately, to write evidence of its presence for their self-assessment.

The descriptive statements within our Narrative Outline and PQI were stated as "don'ts," and the teacher candidates added "don't dominate conversations and do not monopolize the class or group discussion." However, it was interesting to note that they expressed most goals in positive language, such as "putting aside personal feelings if someone accidentally oversteps language boundaries," "agreeing to disagree on controversial topics," "showing flexibility in your own opinions and ideas," "allowing an individual to finish a verbal statement without interrupting or judging," "praising ideas given from others," and "bringing it [need for respect] to others' attention when needed." It was refreshing for us to hear teacher candidates' voices dwell on the positive manifestations of respect. We are working diligently to absorb this perspective as our own.

Reflection is an elusive concept for many students, and is one that requires discussion, teacher modeling, and practice in order to be addressed effectively by the teacher candidates. The conceptual framework in our teacher education department states that a reflective practitioner is one of the desired outcomes for the program. However, bringing teacher candidates to an understanding of the reflective process is a major undertaking (Grossman, 1990; La-Boskey, 1994).

As we critiqued this disposition, our teacher candidates had several suggestions for descriptors that prompted thoughtful discussion and elaboration. They felt that evidence of reflective behavior could include "connecting past experiences to subject matter," "determining ways in which the content of the day could be applied to future teaching and content area," "comparing class to the field experience," and "possibly admitting to a change in misconceptions and schemata."

Our teacher candidates seem to feel that *professionalism* is a distant goal because they are still students and have no extensive experience with the context of the public school classroom and the school environment in general. They indicated that a transition from student to teacher is gradual; it could not be forced or expected to occur just because graduation was only a semester away. Therefore, they testified, student behavior was still the norm and teacher behavior was sporadic. How would they write descriptors for professionalism? They hadn't lived it yet!

We encouraged them to think in terms of professional behavior in the university classroom and how it would be recognized. One teacher candidate seemed to cover all the bases by saying, "Be an exemplar of the field." Others suggested "thinking before you speak," "being able to receive criticism from teacher or peers without reacting in a defensive or negative manner," "using refined language [I mean don't use youth casual language]," and "showing leadership and preparedness to facilitate learning."

Of all of the disposition categories, *listening* would allegedly be one that our teacher candidates believed they had mastered over years of classroom experience. However, they did note a significant difference between hearing what is transpiring in a discussion and actually listening. They expressed concern that the very techniques they might have used to "fake" listening would be those used by their future students. Our teacher candidates expressed concern that listening is not an observable behavior because there is no way of proving that it is occurring unless the listener offers feedback that shows engagement. One candidate succinctly called listening "silent learning" and felt that it was not readily discernible.

To raise their own awareness of the essential role of listening from the speaker's reference point, they declared characteristics of active listening should be added to the rubric descriptors. The descriptors would address the demonstration of active listening through nonverbal behaviors, for example, head nodding, eye contact, and facial expressions. Again, knowing that these can be artificial, overt actions that do not necessarily represent active listening, our teacher candidates felt that professionalism should be their watchdog. A couple suggested that "motivated note-taking" by listeners may be evidence of an engaged learner and listener.

Even though our teacher candidates indicated throughout the analysis process of the instruments that specific descriptors should be added and deleted, we have not necessarily altered the written text of our assessment. We believe that most of their critiques and concerns required adjustments in the presentation of our instruments rather than a change in the language itself. The requests for clarity of language and specific examples were addressed through creative and thorough instruction during the initial presentation as well as at intervals throughout the first three to five sessions. The concept of teacher dispositions and our instruments are too much to grasp in an initial exposure, so we have learned that repetition and chunking produce greater understanding in our teacher candidates.

As a result of hindsight, we recognize that there are viable suggestions for changes to the descriptors and a discussion of the application of the descriptors that is sensitive to learning styles and culture. Why have we made so few formal changes to our instruments? Do we solicit our teacher candidates' input with the intention of confirming our instrument and making changes or do we go through the process merely to make them feel as if they are contributing in order to facilitate buy-in? Or is it a little bit of both? Is it enough to add written changes resulting from discussion during a specific semester? Must every single suggestion be added to subsequent PQIs to prove we value student input?

RUMINATIONS

Since using our PQI, the in-your-face response—"Who do you think you are . . . ?"—to assessing teacher dispositions has disappeared. We believe that as we include our teacher candidates' voices, validate their prior knowledge and experiences, and show where these align (and do not align) with research, their openness to engage in the process increases. By taking teacher candidates' practice and showing how it fits (or does not fit) with existing research, we are able to show that they already have a place in the theoretical world. We then ask them to be more systematic and intentional with something that they take for granted—how their teacher dispositions are personified in the public context. Sounds obvious, but apparently it was not.

The next chapter is devoted to the exploration of what teacher candidates see in themselves as they become more systematic and intentional with teacher dispositions. Their insights often provide endearing portraits of individuals actively engaged in molding and shaping their teacher identity. There are also portraits of those who seem disengaged from or disinterested in this process, which is disconcerting, at best. As we strive to make sense of a multitude of voices, our reflections on the definition, role, and assessment of teacher dispositions continue. Guess we'll never be "done."

Chapter Three

What Do Teacher Candidates See while in Our University Courses?

Kelley prepared to turn in the personal qualitative inventory (PQI) at midterm. The gamut of thoughts and emotions experienced since those opening days of the semester, when the concept of dispositions was dumped on the class, stimulated the following internal soliloquy: *Leave it to education to coin another word that is going to give me more hoops to jump through before I can get the diploma and finally do the "real" work of teaching kids. Well, it's not so bad. At first I didn't know what to write, but the descriptors and the encouragement from the professor helped me to focus on my behaviors and thoughts. I think I did a pretty good job inventorying my personal reactions to the context and dynamics of the classroom. I thought I knew what listening and respect were, but when I really paid attention to what I was doing they seemed different to me; now I seem to look at cause and effect, not just whether or not I am doing it.*

Three days later . . . the professor returns the PQI to each of the teacher candidates with annotations. Kelley reads the comments and thinks, *Wow! Given what the professor said, she sees me like I am intending her to see me. This is great! It feels good to be confirmed in my self-perceptions. There is only one category where we do not see eye-to-eye and that is professionalism. I am really not surprised that the bulk of her questions and comments are in that category. I am not*

> *clear what that looks like, especially in my university class-*
> *room with my peers. I think I will look at her comments and*
> *see if they spark some thoughts and, if not, I may have to visit*
> *with her to get some clarification.*

So far in our journey, we have experienced multiple opportunities to contemplate, elaborate, inform, listen, modify, and question. We also felt joy, disappointment, confusion, anger, euphoria, and disbelief. The earliest instruments that we used played an essential role in the saga of identifying, describing, and assessing the dispositions we selected as foci for our teacher candidates. As precursors for the *personal qualitative inventory* (PQI), they helped us realize the importance of creating an instrument that invited student voices into the process of self-realization. We determined that our teacher candidates needed to write about dispositions on an intrapersonal level in order to "see" themselves as they experienced a process of recognition, application, and interpretation.

Brookfield (1995) supports our decision to invite the teacher candidates to write, as explicitly as they can, what they are experiencing in their thoughts and actions. He acknowledges that this "critical reflection entails all kinds of risks and complexities" (p. 22). In addition, such autobiographical writing provides a lens through which to view ourselves and reveal assumptions (beliefs that are taken for granted) that may frame how we think and act. Palmer (1998) talks about teacher identity and how the authority of inner life comes to teachers from "authoring their own words, their own actions, their own lives, rather than playing a scripted role" (p. 33). Through the process of writing about their personal dispositions, we believe teacher candidates stand a better chance of weaving positive teacher dispositions into their emerging teacher identity.

This chapter focuses on how teacher candidates used the reflective writing process to explore teacher dispositions within themselves. You will "hear" their voices as they hold up a mirror, think about the dispositions they see reflected, and then craft these thoughts into words focused specifically on their university classroom interactions.

In chapter 4, we examine the insights from their PQIs recorded during their clinical field experiences within K–12 classrooms. As we "listen" to their voices, we seek to understand how our teacher candidates define, identify, and work with the dispositions we selected: What do they see in themselves? What influence, if any, does the process have on their developing teacher identity?

At one level, the voices of our teacher candidates speak for themselves. At another level, as teacher educators, we feel an obligation to interpret the messages to foster continuous learning on teacher dispositions. We invite you to make meaning from these insights as well and to consider the possibility that these voices could echo in your classrooms. We realize that your contexts may differ greatly from ours, which will obviously alter any use of our processes. As a result, your teacher candidates' voices may sound dissimilar, leading you to interpretations most appropriate for your context. Having said that, we do feel that the heart of a teacher usually beats with a similar rhythm regardless of the context in which it resides. So, we believe you will benefit from hearing the voices of our teacher candidates.

As mentioned earlier, this chapter contains the voices of our teacher candidates as they worked with teacher dispositions within the context of our university classrooms. After providing you with some contextual background, we present teacher candidates' voices associated with each of our six dispositions: continuous learning, cooperation and collaboration, listening, respect, professionalism, and reflection. As their thinking processes unfold, you will recognize comments that range from the blasé to the profound. We hope you connect with both the processes our teacher candidates experienced and the insights they share.

UNIVERSITY CLASSROOM CONTEXT

We and the teacher candidates experienced disposition learning and documentation simultaneously. As they kept themselves under a personal watchful eye and inventoried their dispositions within the context of our university classrooms, we anxiously anticipated reading the entries in their PQIs. We did not know what to expect. However, we hoped that as a result of what we read in the PQIs and witnessed during the ensuing class discussions, the concept of teacher dispositions would become clearer to us and to our teacher candidates. Through their documentation, we were learning how they identified dispositions. Consequently, we honed our skill for encouraging them to scrutinize their dispositions and then articulate what they saw. We were all involved in a cyclical process that was not necessarily synchronized.

Lest you think that we are presenting a fairy tale for consumption, please be assured that we experienced resistance. Resistance came in the form of voices shared aloud as well as in writing: "I do not like to journal." "I am not a writer." "I don't know how to think about things deeply." "I do not know what to write; what do you want?" "It is hard for me to remember what I did and then label it."

Then, when some of our teacher candidates recorded entries, they would limit their comments to phrases that were superficial or did not retain meaning if they were separated from the intended category: "Kept my opinions to myself"; "Concept of vocabulary"; "Participated in group dialogue." We felt that this indicated a resistance to engaging in the process of self-discovery and possibly a way of passively enduring the request to record evidence on dispositions. These reactions, as well as others, are evident in the subsequent sections of this chapter.

CONTINUOUS LEARNING

One of the most common foci for teacher candidates is to list new information presented in class and to comment on whether it confirmed or challenged their previous knowledge and experiences. Hear what these six teacher candidates (TCs) have to say:

Lesson about barriers to new learning was a good review. (TC 57)

I learned a lot about the Anticipation Guides, and I will definitely use them in the field and on the job. (TC 58)

I learned new strategies that will help me as a teacher, for example, direct instruction. (TC 21)

Learned new strategies to incorporate vocabulary into my content area. (TC 8)

Already knew about [multiple intelligences], and I had a hard time focusing because it was repetitive. (TC 15)

I believe I was able to learn about concepts that I had not been exposed to with other education classes. By discussing topics like integrity and identity, capacity for connectedness and other topics expanded my knowledge about certain teacher attributes, especially ones that make a teacher great. (TC 46)

As we attempt to make meaning out of these PQI entries, we are confounded by their superficial nature. Teacher candidates merely list or describe events happening in our university classrooms.

Our goal is always to promote critical reflection on information presented in class and to encourage assessment of the value of particular strategies or concepts. We would like the inner voices of our teacher candidates to ask, Why is this information new? What is the rationale for this strategy? Why would I use it or not use it? Do I believe this concept will help me be a more effective teacher? We do not expect our teacher candidates to banter naturally with their inner voices, but we would like them to become comfortable with the metacognitive process while considering adoption of new information. We look for movement from literal understanding to evaluation and eventually synthesis of new ideas with their prior knowledge. Teacher candidates' progress toward ownership of new information requires finding harmony between that information and their budding teacher identities. Some teacher candidates did move beyond superficial descriptions of class interactions:

> I learned a different lesson plan than the one I am used to and made myself think of benefits instead of being crabby about having to do things differently. (TC 4)

> Today I learned about graphic organizers. I must admit I was not excited about them at first. However, exchanging ideas with my partner gave me a new perspective on their usefulness. (TC 53)

> Today I exhibited continuous learning by revisiting the concepts of literacy and schema. During the class discussion, I thought about my prior knowledge regarding these topics and also added to the concepts by identifying how schemata works for students in their learning process. (TC 60)

These teacher candidates exhibit characteristics related to being open minded and flexible. Although they started with a mere descriptor of the lesson's content, they were inspired to consider the ramifications of this content to their own teaching or learning situations. One teacher candidate was open to and flexible with not only content but also her teacher identity and the context within which it lives:

> In addition, I realized that just as an independent learner is always becoming, as a teacher I am also becoming; continuously learning about myself, subject matter, and students. (TC 46)

Self-discovery is also evident among other teacher candidates:

> Today we learned about the learning cycle. Professor Jenkins said that we not only have to know the learning cycle, we have to teach it. This was an epiphany in that I am not only learning something for a test; I want to know it for my teaching skills. Kind of learning for the sake of learning! (TC 34)

> Have started to think more along the lines of what can I get out of this rather than why do I need to do this. . . . Instead of just wanting to

know what others think, I want to know why it is they think that way—what factors have influenced their opinion? (TC 45)

The activities involving vocabularies today allowed me to understand the depth of involvement and creativity that goes into preparing lesson plans. I felt extremely creative in developing and learning about these approaches to teaching vocabulary, but at the same time realized that I will be humbled, more than once, when giving my students something I created. (TC 14)

By writing our Teacher Identity papers, it forced me, in a way, to dig deep and just think about why I want to teach. I think I learn more about myself and my family when I reflect on this kind of assignment. (TC 71)

These written entries convey to us the power behind using written reflection to name and claim teacher dispositions. Our teacher candidates recognized elements in themselves that were not a part of their teacher identity prior to thinking about classroom experiences in light of *continuous learning*.

Yet another teacher candidate wrote, "Learned a lot today. I continue to learn information pertaining to the education field." This entry made us chuckle. We saw humor in the fact that this teacher candidate felt compelled to tell us he was learning education concepts in an education course. In addition to laughing at such statements, we admonished ourselves for opportunities missed.

Another teacher candidate wrote, "I agree that we are forever continuous learners." As it stands, this statement is philosophically sound, but in a superficial way—stating the obvious without demonstrating application. We gave written feedback that encouraged this teacher candidate to explore how and why this would manifest itself in her teaching and learning experiences. However, time worked against us, and we were unable to further nurture her thinking regarding this disposition. We wonder how many other opportunities we missed, and think about how we can be more proactive in the future. This provides further evidence that teachers at all levels need to engage in continuous learning.

COOPERATION AND COLLABORATION

The teacher candidates talked about *cooperation and collaboration* as something they experienced many times in their university classrooms. They had numerous opportunities to do group work, which was identified as cooperative learning, and felt that collaboration was simply getting the project done with the least amount of pain! After studying cooperative learning from a pedagogical perspective (see Johnson, Johnson, & Holubec, 1998; Kauchak & Eggen, 2003; Ryder & Graves, 2003), this disposition took on deeper and broader meanings. Cooperation and collaboration began to involve processes and products, not merely "getting along" or "giving in for the sake of the group."

> Throughout the group work we have been completing in class, I have realized the importance of open-mindedness and a professional attitude. . . . I have had incredibly beneficial group work periods. . . . I have also worked in groups where close-mindedness and egocentrism were dominant forces. As educators, we have to work to overcome these attitudes and make gains in our professional development amidst the animosity. (TC 14)

When cooperation is coupled with collaboration, this dispositional category necessitates that teacher candidates give more attention to personal responsibility. It also requires them to combine the talents, skills, and energy of each team member, since finished products represent something greater than any single individual's input. The teacher candidates live cooperation and collaboration through course assignments (e.g., Interdisciplinary Team Project and Inquiry into Current Educational Issues) that obligate them to work across subject areas.

Teacher candidates' entries in their PQIs further confirm their growing understanding of cooperation and collaboration:

> Most important day of all in terms of cooperation and collaboration. Hard for five people to plan a group project. Had to let go of things I

thought would be good because there were science and physical education people in the group who had to be considered . . . too many bosses in the beginning. (TC 57)

Preparing for the IDU [interdisciplinary unit] took so much cooperation and collaboration. In fact, it was the most I have ever worked with a group! Our presentation went very smoothly because of that. (TC 59)

I am a very strong leader. Sometimes I think it is good to step back and let others take the lead. This is hard for me to do sometimes, but I believe this will strengthen my teaching skills. (TC 40)

I work much better while in small groups. I am not as shy! Learning to work in groups is a life-long process, and it is an important skill for students [teacher candidates] to learn. (TC 50)

I really enjoyed working and putting this project [IDU] together. I learned a lot about myself as an individual and how to work with different teachers from different subject areas. (TC 51)

My partner had not completed his assignment so I didn't have anything to look at during work time. This shows the interdependence that is needed in cooperative groups. It indicates to me that the dynamic of a group can be changed if all members have not completed their work. (TC 54)

In our IDU team meeting, we were supposed to come up with a topic. I don't believe we did this as a group. I think [two members] came up with it and nobody disagreed. I don't have a problem with the topic. . . . I just don't think we worked well as a team. (TC 71)

Cooperation and collaboration in any context is complex. Yet, initially, teacher candidates believed they had a strong working definition for this disposition. The types of entries they recorded after a lesson on the pedagogy of cooperative learning leads us to believe that we need to be systematic and intentional at an earlier point in the semester about this particular disposition so we can help teacher candidates look at something they believe they understand through a different lens (i.e., make the familiar strange). The use of instructional techniques and activities that afford demonstration and immersion for the teacher candidates bring cooperation and collaboration into the practical realm. This creates a readiness when they encounter the K–12 school context.

Not all teacher candidates relished the opportunity to work on cooperation and collaboration within the context of course assignments, as represented by the following comment:

> After working with colleagues in our group [IDU], I am not sure I like working in groups rather than independently. I feel that group work is a lot more time consuming and it would get done a lot faster independently. It's tough for all people to decide on some things. (TC 72)

One concern proposed by several teacher candidates was whether or not one should ignore, argue, or try to change the behavior of a colleague who is making group work unbearable. Specifically, one candidate asked, "Where does professionalism come into this scenario?" We applaud this question and continue to wrestle with how to word our response professionally. What do you think?

LISTENING

"What do you think we have been doing for over 15 years?" This was the essence of disbelief from teacher candidates that *listening* was a disposition that needed disciplined attention at this point in their teacher preparation. However, as the verbal dust settled, they approached this disposition with an observable sense of confidence that prior experience was going to take care of their concerns about the art of listening.

In many early entries, teacher candidates again recorded short descriptions of their behaviors rather than critically reflecting on them. The descriptions touched on the following topics: listening in large- and small-group settings, listening to the professor, demonstrating active listening behaviors (e.g., head nodding, smiling, eye contact, gestures), questioning to demonstrate engagement, summarizing to confirm intended message, talking less, being patient, connecting listening to comprehension, and note-taking. We viewed these as practical applications of and responses to the art of listening.

At the same time we were enlightened by many voices that revealed a growing maturity:

> Today in small group as I was listening to what everyone was contributing to the group list, I couldn't think of anything else, so I asked the recorder to read off what everyone had added. This way everyone could know if anything else was needed [for clarification]. (TC 42)

> If [someone] is not being listened to and their contributions are not being valued, that person will become frustrated and the effectiveness of the group [small-group activity] will be compromised. (TC 49)

> Not listening at all today! I got very bad news today and was completely distracted. I think I need to work on this; funny—always thought I was a "good" listener. (TC 19)

> Listened in my group, especially the nonverbal cues and body language, as people who didn't know each other all that well were trying to come up with an idea that suited everyone. (TC 57)

Much to our delight, several teacher candidates seem to understand that listening is not a passive act. They stated that there is physical demonstration indicating engagement while listening, and there is a reward system when it is done well (e.g., learning information, feeling good about honoring someone else's sharing, providing feedback that assists others). We think that the teacher candidates truly recognized cognitive, affective, and psychomotor objectives associated with listening.

Through our PQI, we promote listening as a unique disposition with its own identity. In addition to working with listening as a disposition with distinctive descriptors, teacher candidates were able to solidify their understanding of it by recognizing connections between listening and the other five dispositions to which they were attending.

They realized that listening is embedded in or intertwined with these other dispositions. While we too recognize that listening permeates the other dispositions in our PQI, we endorse the idea that it is a disposition that must be explored as a separate entity. Such focused attention increases the chances that it can be effectively transferred for utilization within the other dispositions. Therefore, listening has a single identity and a communal identity.

At times we wonder if our teacher candidates actually realize the messages about teaching and learning that are implied in their PQIs.

> 9/14: Listening today was easy for me because I wrote down others' opinions rather than just listening.
> 9/23: I was able to listen well today because I was interested in people's ways of doing their graphic organizers.
> 10/5: Listening was hard for me today in large group because I am giving a speech later today. It's amazing how you can be taken off-subject. (TC 17)

This sequence of entries from one teacher candidate's PQI helps illustrate what we deem significant influencing factors in K–12 classrooms. There is a strong connection between motivation and listening for this teacher candidate. Will she recognize that the same will be true for future students? Note-taking enhances this teacher candidate's ability to actively listen. Will she share this strategy with future students? External pressures influenced her ability to listen. Will she take this into consideration when observing future students' classroom behaviors?

Most teacher candidates were not able to make these connections. We saw the value of bringing potential connections to the forefront during classroom discussions. Working with dispositions became an avenue for talking about classroom environment, instructional strategies, and other teacher preparation topics. Our intent was to demonstrate how their personal experiences with dispositions could transfer to the context of the K–12 classroom. You can judge the extent to which we were successful in this arena as you read chapter 4.

RESPECT

There were virtually no narrative comments pertaining to *respect* until the semester we started using the PQI. With the PQI firmly in place, teacher candidates' narrations tied respect to good listening techniques, to sensitivity for others, and to honoring suggestions and criticism from peers. Like listening, it appears to have both a single and communal identity. Still other candidates approached respect in all-encompassing ways. One candidate wrote,

> I don't think there is any word any more important than the word *respect* when it comes to teaching. The most important kind of respect is the respect teachers should always have for students. This should set the stage for the respect students should have for one another and for their teacher . . . kindness is very much like respect. (TC 57)

Another teacher candidate shared ideas about respect in the following creative way:

> I thought of an acronym for RESPECT and figured this would be a good venue to archive it [in the PQI] till I'm actually in the classroom:
>
> R = responsible
> E = educated
> S = students
> P = promoting
> E = ethical
> C = conduct
> T = together (TC 63)

Many references to respect, as it manifested itself in our university classrooms, centered on partner and group work. Examples from these contexts include the following:

> A part of being respectful is participating actively [in class or in groups]. (TC 59)

I have gained new respect for my group [IDU team] because I was able to witness other people's preparedness. (TC 6)

As I go on I feel my respect growing for others [peers in the course]. I mean I had respect as we came in, but it has grown now that I know about my constituents more, which allows me to open up more and share my ideas. (TC 39)

I found myself wanting to interrupt people in their arguments but catching myself because just because I disagree does not mean that they don't have a valid point. That is really part of learning. (TC 68)

These exemplars seem to promote a perception of respect that falls within a broad interpretation of the concept—active participation, attention to the efforts of others, and openness to varied opinions.

However, we are reminded of the multiple definitions that can be attributed to a disposition by the following excerpts from one individual's PQI:

- I thought that person's reasons for teaching were strange, but didn't say anything.
- I was nice about the partner forgetting guide even though it left me with nothing to do.
- I listened well about a book that I had read and did not like but did not say so because this person really liked it.
- I listened to everyone's examples even though I am sick of it. (TC 41)

This teacher candidate's perception differed from the more broad interpretations previously outlined. The comments made over the course of the semester have a ring of cynicism to them that was unsuccessfully veiled as displays of respect.

Comparatively, some teacher candidates did demonstrate apparent positive change over the course of the semester. In this example, the teacher candidate moves from a tongue-in-cheek response to one that seems more thoughtful:

2/4: Deciding on a topic for IDU required that I acknowledge each person's ideas as having some value. I was able to do this "gracefully."

4/21: I have a new attitude about receiving feedback from peers. I can discuss suggestions and offer suggestions and not take them personally. (TC 53)

In this next example, a different teacher candidate moved from personal goal setting to a statement of confirmation:

2/11: I need to be aware of and do a better job at waiting for someone else to stop talking before I start talking. . . .

4/21: I know that my views could be beneficial to my class, but I don't always have to expose them. (TC 61)

The context of speaking to and interacting with their peers also provided intriguing insights into the complexities of respect for teacher candidates. At the end of each semester, they made in-class presentations, which stimulated the following testimonies:

I tried to make eye contact as well as ask questions to ensure the presenters that I was listening. When my classmates give me respect while I present, it makes me feel like I did a better job. (TC 50)

During the first day of our presentations, I saw several classmates of mine looking down, looking bored, or even working on other materials while groups presented their work. I find this behavior very disrespectful to the presenters. This behavior is very surprising considering that the people not paying attention will soon be the people up in front of the class. I wonder if they consider that when choosing their own behaviors. Of course, most of the class paid close attention and valued the speakers. It is those people whom I respect. (TC 49)

There are times when you just are not impressed with work from people [your peers]. It is these times when respect is most needed. I find it hard to watch and listen to people who don't put their *all* into their work. (TC 10)

These particular testimonies demonstrate recognition of the power of nonverbal communication. Teacher candidates were tuned in to both the positive and negative aspects of their peers' demeanor and seemed inclined to view respect as reciprocal—to get it, you have to give it.

Rarely, if ever, did anyone write about respect for us as their Secondary Block professors. It seems that our teacher candidates focused solely on dispositions as they applied to themselves and their developing teacher identities. We worked diligently to help them transition from student to teacher and to recognize each other as colleagues. Somewhere along the way, they forgot our role in this educational environment.

When teacher candidates considered respect as it manifests itself in the university classroom, their interactions with us that depicted the teacher–student relationship did not appear in their PQI entries. Conversely, when they entered their K–12 field experience, their PQI entries often focused on the teacher–student relationship. These entries included not only their nascent teacher relationship with students but their cooperating teachers' relationships with students as well. Finally, they discussed their relationship with their cooperating teachers. Chapter 4 elaborates on these experiences.

PROFESSIONALISM

Of all the dispositions in the PQI entries, those associated with *professionalism* are the most challenging for us, as teacher educators, to read. The primary reason for this is that the entries defied neat categorization. Since our Secondary Block is last in the teacher education program, just prior to student teaching, we assumed that our teacher candidates would be more attuned to the attributes of professionalism in an educational setting. A few demonstrated some acuity with this disposition: "It's important at this stage of the game to make the transition from student to teacher" and "It's time to act like an adult!"

Others continued to puzzle over just what professionalism looked like in a university classroom. The conundrum surrounding professionalism was adeptly expressed by one teacher candidate:

> How can you measure professionalism? I see it in enthusiasm, work ethic, and general tendency to do a great job? Being professional is something that is a result of doing the "other" things well. I think everyone needs to realize that we all are professionals. We must all be accountable for ourselves . . . take pride in everything we do and produce. . . . I am reconfirmed that our educational society is made up of many professionals. (TC 74)

This teacher candidate's comments suggest that professionalism should permeate all that we do in classrooms. However, having said this, our teacher candidates reported that they found it very difficult to identify professional behavior while still in the university classroom. Their assertion that their teacher identities were in the early stages of development contributed to their inability to work with this disposition. In addition, they viewed respect and cooperation and collaboration as related areas to professionalism, so earmarking entries as solely professionalism was problematic. Here again, teacher candidates are confronted with a disposition that has a communal identity.

While in the university classroom, common themes among their professionalism entries included having patience with peers, being prepared, keeping groups on task, showing respectful consideration for contributions to group function, assimilating elements of what peers said into their own beliefs, and assessing peer work with honesty. We hear additional insights reflected in the following excerpts:

> I find it's easy to be professional if you agree with someone! (TC 10)

> I'm learning . . . that it is more difficult to work with teachers in other subjects than I thought it was going to be. (TC 15)

Teacher candidates came into our Secondary Block with a certain amount of naiveté. They had not been asked to contemplate seriously teacher dispositions in their previous teacher education courses. Hence, there was a certain level of idealism in their initial thinking. When they were required to ponder how our selected dispositions manifested themselves in our university classrooms, they discovered the complex nature of teacher dispositions.

For some, learning from the curriculum shared in the university classroom, be it explicit or implicit, demonstrated a commitment to professionalism: "For my students, I would like to have many different vocabulary teaching styles mastered. I believe they would see me as a professional teacher if I could meet their many learning styles," and "Professionalism was shown today when we reworked the course syllabus for the remainder of the semester. We planned the assignments and papers with corresponding due dates. This showed concern [by the professor] with quality work and flexibility in scheduling."

At the end of the semester, our teacher candidates wrote how professionalism did not become truly evident to them until they were in the public school context and felt the impact of expectations from students, cooperating teachers, administrators, parents, and other stakeholders. The various responses outlined above remind us that evolving identities require teacher candidates to find an integration of who they are as persons, students, and budding teachers. All of these identities have unique components, yet they flow into each other and feed the aura of professionalism.

REFLECTION

While teacher candidates' struggle with *professionalism* caught us off-guard, we had anticipated that they would grapple with *reflection*. Our College of Education's Conceptual Framework asserts that teacher candidates should be Reflective Practitioners. In fact, the phrase from our Conceptual Framework most recognized by teacher candidates in the program is Reflective Practitioners. This rhetoric tends to look good on paper, to make sense cognitively, and to rest close to the heartbeat of what is desired in the ideal candidate. However, *reflection* often becomes intangible in the world of hands-on teaching and learning. Can you teach someone to reflect, and how do they know when they are reflecting? We trudged on, doing our best to clarify this concept and hoping that our teacher candidates would do the same.

Our teacher candidates seemed to wrestle cognitively with the appropriate words to use to articulate reflection. Initially, they used the exact language of the descriptors (refer to appendix 3). Teacher candidates also struggled with the affective domain. A vast array of emotions such as discovery, acceptance, and exasperation are mirrored in the following comments:

> As I reflected upon my reflection today, I realized how important it is to reflect. (TC 57)

> Anytime or every day that I make an entry in this PQI, I am honing my skills on reflection. (TC 69)

> Between the IDU [interdisciplinary unit], journal responses, SST [social studies methods course] work, I totally do not have sufficient time to produce even half-assed lesson plans . . . time management is crucial. . . . I am no longer using any time to do these reflections. I have too many other things I have to do. (TC 18)

Our verbal elaboration and written feedback (hearken back to chapter 2) combined with teacher candidates' persistence enabled many to experience considerable growth in their ability to reflect:

> Today was an opportunity to reevaluate my thoughts on teaching techniques. In our groups we discussed learning strategies. Thinking back to my education, this was an opportunity to compare old ideas and new ideas. (TC 53)

> When doing the multiple intelligences readings, I asked myself what are my strengths and weaknesses. It makes me wonder if I can teach students whose strengths are my weaknesses. (TC 44)

Took it upon myself to reflect on the comments I gave to see if I was truly being honest with myself and others. (TC 65)

As we keep discussing different strategies to get kids to read, I keep thinking to myself, this is also directed to me. I have similar problems when I read, such as staying focused, comprehension, and reading for enjoyment. (TC 71)

These compelling examples of reflection show relevance between theory and practice as they come together in teacher candidates' lived experiences. Through reflection, teacher candidates systematically examine their classroom experiences, make connections to who they are or want to be as teachers, and find ways to foster their teacher identity. In this process, they bring past, present, and future together in meaningful ways. What more could we ask from reflection!

RUMINATIONS

What we discovered was that individual linear growth from the first entry to the last was rare. The teacher candidates seemed to write a random collection of behaviors and thoughts with each disposition, spontaneously interacting with and making meaning of the university classroom context and its dynamics. The entries generally did not follow a pattern from good, to better, to best as the weeks unfolded. Instead, the quality of the entries depended on the power of the classroom context to stimulate a personalized experience that hit a cognitive and/or affective nerve. Therefore, we were not inclined to look for developmental growth within each candidate's entries as much as to watch for the epiphanies that would occur in whatever order.

Instead of taking a deep breath and thinking "so what?" when the teacher candidates would write entries that contained information that we thought they should have been aware of long ago, we learned to celebrate with them these self-revelations of even the minutest growth. We discovered that the sooner we could appreciate the potential for serious reflection and response from our teacher candidates that had no obvious order but did demonstrate movement, the sooner multiple voices would be heard and valued for their hidden, insightful gems. This reconfirmed for us the complexity of the world of education.

Our appreciation for potential also reinforced for us, as teacher educators, that growth and development in teacher dispositions may not occur in a linear fashion. Teacher candidates may advance in unexpected ways, traversing winding, untraveled paths. We need to be patient, content, and accepting of this process.

In this chapter, we shared a portion of our teacher candidates' voices that we were fortunate to read and study via their PQIs. These excerpts were recorded while they were immersed in our university classrooms, interacting with each other and us, their professors. Before they went into their K–12 field experience, we suggested that the change of context might offer a different perspective of and experience with each of the dispositions. Did this happen? Read on and see.

Chapter Four

What Do Teacher Candidates See while in K–12 Classrooms?

Kelley sits back in contemplation: *Wow! When I think back to the teaching I observed and the lessons I taught over the past few weeks, I hear the voices of my professors during the orientation session. They said that the new context of the field experience may play a significant role in how I would experience and view dispositions. In fact, that may be why I am experiencing all this confusion, excitement, wonderment, and anticipation as I sit down to write in my personal qualitative inventory. All of these emotions are coming at the same time.*

Further thoughts abound: *Yes, continuous learning seems to be a daily task in order to absorb the new context of a K–12 classroom and all of its dynamics, including the school as a whole. All the dispositions feel different here, so this must be the progress and growth that we talked about in the university classroom.* Putting pen to paper, Kelley begins to record evidences of various dispositions as they look, feel, and sound in this new setting.

"I can't wait to get out there and work with the students"; we hear this mantra from teacher candidates as they anticipate the starting date of their six-week field experience. This is what they spent years preparing for, sitting in university classrooms and trying to envision the implementation of all that they have learned. Their enthusiasm is contagious as they share their eagerness to begin living the "real" world of teaching.

We are as excited as our teacher candidates; however, our excitement is tempered by the realization that we need to practice restraint, not dictating to or interpreting for them their future classroom experiences. Our own personal public school experiences occurred in particular contexts and were influenced by all the players in that space. Our teacher candidates deserve the opportunity to interpret their experiences with their context and players as it applies to their emerging teacher identities. It challenges our dispositions to remain relevant to them as sources of information and guidance while trying to release them into this world of application.

The field experience takes place in a context with different features and dynamics than our university classrooms. Students, faculty, support staff, administration, and parents engage in complex interactions within a structured workday infused with extracurricular activities and wrapped up in current accountability issues. Although they experienced this context as students, their new role as teacher candidates will offer them an opportunity to attain an expanded perspective on these dynamics. We try to foreshadow some of these differences, stimulating thoughts about the potential impact of this new context on the development of their knowledge, skills, and dispositions. During the orientation session for the field experience, we explore with teacher candidates the logistics of negotiating the policies and politics that permeate the K–12 setting.

In the university classroom, the teacher candidates become familiar with how our selected dispositions posited themselves, so writing about them becomes situated within their comfort zones. We know that the K–12 setting will provide multiple and diverse experiences within which these dispositions will take on new appearances. The teacher candidates receive this information with a mixture of disbelief and a sense of the obvious. Their nonverbal communication usually says, "Duh, we know it's not the same context."

At this point in time, it works to our advantage to assume the parenting role. We know that sometimes children will not believe what their parents tell them, and it is best to have them experience something rather than force vicarious understanding. So we just sit back and let our teacher candidates enter their field experience with the knowledge that we are available as a support system.

For the most part, the *personal qualitative inventory* (PQI) entries made by our teacher candidates during the field experiences support our prediction that they would experience teacher dispositions differently in the context of the K–12 classroom than they did in our university classrooms. Here again we seek to understand how our teacher candidates define, identify, and work with our selected dispositions in the context of their field experience—What do they see in themselves? What influence, if any, does the process have on their developing teacher identity? Does their attention to dispositions influence their decisions as teachers?

The voices of our teacher candidates still speak for themselves. However, we continue to interpret the messages to broaden the conversation on teacher dispositions. Questions for you to ponder during your reading include, but are not limited to: Can teacher dispositions transcend theory to practice? How do you help prepare teacher candidates to enter the K–12 environment?

CONTINUOUS LEARNING

Our teacher candidates consistently stated their belief that lifelong learning is part of the teaching profession. It seemed like a cliché that had lost its meaning through overuse and assumption. However, this cliché was turned on its side as our teacher candidates became actively engaged with *continuous learning* in their new K–12 contexts.

> One of the big lessons I learned at my site was that teaching is continuous learning. So many of the things my CT taught were things I

had never studied, or never studied enough to teach. I don't think it matters how long you've been teaching—I think you continue to learn. I had to read two books and do research just to keep up with what was going on in class to teach my unit. I had to research an entire area and plan the paperwork, lectures, and activities. If this isn't continuous learning, I don't know what is! (TC 57)

My field experience is going well. I feel I've learned more in these three-and-a-half weeks than I have during any other three-week span of my life. There has been a lot of continuous learning happening as I watch my teacher . . . viewing many of the concepts previously taught to me being modeled. I feel I have just begun the process of becoming a great teacher because there is so much to continually learn. (TC 77)

This field experience has basically been one huge continuous learning experience! I have been forced to rethink a great number of my preconceptions re: education . . . from the relative importance of content, personal relationships, etc. . . . . to discipline methods, scheduling, and lesson planning. (TC 4)

These voices illustrate a newfound awareness of the awesome task of teaching. Learning came to be defined differently. When they entered the K–12 classroom and took on teacher responsibilities, learning was no longer just for themselves. As a teacher, many more people depended on their depth of understanding and their ability to make it comprehensible to students with a variety of learning styles and needs. Our teacher candidates recognized that it was necessary to look at and study materials differently in order to be ready to facilitate student understanding. The art of teaching looked dissimilar in real time to what it did on the written page or in memory. They began to revisit their initial perceptions of teaching and learning.

By the end of the field experience, some of our candidates suggested that they needed to give continuous learning more attention:

I think I could develop my continuous learning. . . . Deep down inside I realize I can never know enough material, but sometimes I feel I can get by. (TC 77)

I think continuous learning stood out [as needing development] in that there were some questions I still couldn't answer. (TC 4)

Wow! The last few weeks have really taught me how much teachers really need to know about what they are teaching. There is no way you can just "wing it." For this reason I believe continuous learning is even more important than I ever did before. (TC 78)

For some of our teacher candidates, continuous learning took on different characteristics in the field experience than what was experienced in the university classroom, especially with attention to the role of a teacher and the concept of accountability. For others, this disposition became a wake-up call, announcing the need to add to their knowledge base in order to avoid the "fly by the seat of my pants" mentality.

COOPERATION AND COLLABORATION

As presented in chapter 3, our teacher candidates were confident that they had had copious experiences with *cooperation and collaboration* because of the frequent use of cooperative learning in their university classrooms. Again, the K–12 field experience offered a different lens for them to explore this disposition. Some teacher candidates felt the aura that cooperation and collaboration creates in a broader school context:

I feel like this entire profession revolves around collaboration. Teachers need to share ideas and methods so that the entire schooling process will be successful. A successful teacher has a collection of "copied" lessons. It is the personal touch that becomes important when teaching these shared ideas. (TC 74)

I had a unique opportunity in my field to team-teach. . . . It did show me how ideas need to be shared and modified—it doesn't mean your ideas are not good. (TC 53)

Cooperation and collaboration—not only with fellow teachers but also with students—proved to be an area needing further attention. As you likely recognize, I have a tendency to jump out front as a leader in planning, discussion, etc, and while this often is beneficial, I am recognizing there are times when dropping back a bit and compromising more frequently would be very beneficial. (TC 46)

I used to think cooperation and collaboration was a good thing and I still do but in my field experience I saw it working against itself. For this to work, the professionals involved need to give and take and share fully within all reason. (TC 66)

The teacher candidates listed several new situations involving cooperating teachers that required cooperation and collaboration. One candidate eloquently stated,

Cooperation and collaboration have been of paramount importance in the field experience. . . . We [cooperating teacher and teacher candidate] were often forced to compromise on content or discipline so as to both be on the same page—such compromise was much preferred over the appearance of a lack of collaboration, which would have guaranteed failure! (TC 22)

Another teacher candidate seemed to experience this disposition at the "gut level" the first day of teaching in the field:

This one [cooperation and collaboration] was definitely felt my first day of teaching. I had no idea how to keep groups on task. Then my cooperating teacher gave me some pointers and she saved my life. I was utterly lost and hopeless that first day. Thank God she saw that and chimed in like bells from heaven. (TC 14)

The first teacher candidate exuded a sense of entitlement, using the word "compromise" as if he and the cooperating teacher were on equal ground as they contemplated content and discipline. Our initial thoughts were "Lucky you that your cooperating teacher was willing to compromise!" Our experience is that cooperating teachers usually reserve the right to control content and discipline within their classroom. Relinquishing full control of these two areas, in our opinion, was a significant overture on the part of the cooperating teacher. In contrast, the second teacher candidate seemed to emanate gratitude and an appreciation for the mentorship role practiced and performed by the cooperating teacher. The disposition of collaboration and cooperation was viewed differently by these two teacher candidates.

The teacher candidates also spoke of promoting cooperation and collaboration among and with their students as part of establishing classroom atmosphere or completing specific academic tasks:

Walking around during science lab activities made me appreciate and understand the purpose of group work and cooperation. (TC 37)

I divided the class up into the six branches [of the United Nations] and completed Jigsaw 1. This was a very interesting and tough activity [for ninth-grade civics]. Overall, the cooperation of the students allowed us to finish the lesson with the right knowledge base. (TC 38)

One part of cooperation that I have found vital during my field is to cooperate with students. It goes without saying with regard to cooperating with colleagues, but flexibility and cooperation with students is often overlooked. I made an effort to monitor this in myself and liked my progress. (TC 10)

Today I did a jigsaw with the 12th-graders and I learned that it is important to establish group roles. Some of the students did not participate as much as others. Also, by walking around the room, the groups tend to stay on task more often. (TC 11)

While many teacher candidates saw students successfully engage in cooperative and collaborative activities, one did wrestle with applying this disposition. Of primary concern was how best to facilitate student comfort, realizing the sensitivity levels connected to cooperation and collaboration:

> One thing that has not surprised me is that some students love working together while others completely avoid it. I have difficulties knowing how to handle this situation. . . . I have tried organizing students and tasks in such a way as to alleviate the discomfort [feeling left out] but feel as though no matter how I do it I fail and someone feels left out. (TC 47)

This was echoed by another teacher candidate who was working in a classroom for English language learners (ELLs). Sounding frustrated, he wrote,

> The most difficult part of collaborating with students to achieve a goal has been working with those who do not want to work. These students have many different reasons for being unmotivated (frustration with the language barrier, no previous schooling experience, separation from family members, etc.) and it has been difficult to encourage them to do their work. (TC 52)

Cooperation and collaboration manifested itself in much more complex ways within the K–12 context. In our university classroom, teacher candidates planned lessons, talked about discipline, and shared ideas with their peers. Yet those things seemed like a new phenomenon when they worked in the K–12 classroom. Planning lessons, talking about discipline, and sharing ideas with the cooperating teacher took on different characteristics in this new context.

One of the potential benefits of systematically and intentionally thinking about your dispositions, in this case cooperation and collaboration, is that it helps teacher candidates progress in developing their teacher identity. This same phenomenon, experiencing what is thought to be known in a different context and realizing it changes, also holds true with the disposition of listening.

LISTENING

Our teacher candidates took their *listening* adeptness for granted in the early weeks of their university classroom experience. As their semester progressed, however, they grew to respect the receptive and expressive complexity couched within the art of listening, especially as the communication patterns with their peers evolved. The K–12 context, in turn, added new dimensions to the art of listening.

In general, teacher candidates started recognizing previous patterns in their listening that were ineffective, if not detrimental, in the classroom context:

> This has been a skill that I have attempted to develop throughout my college career, and I found myself jumping into conversations and interrupting when I should be listening and giving the students a chance to talk. (TC 10)

> Learning to listen to students is different because you need to listen very carefully and make sure that you don't misinterpret what they say. (TC 23)

> Listening is the part of my dispositions that will need continuous training. I know that I hear my students, but I get angry at myself when I tell them to repeat themselves. (TC 5)

Specifically, the teacher candidates found they were listening attentively to their cooperating teachers, respecting the years of experience that they drew upon:

> The first two weeks of field were spent observing and listening to the cooperating teacher and the students. I tried to actively listen and ask questions whenever possible. I think this is a big part of continuous learning, also. (TC 34)

> I really worked on my listening during my practicum. I was in a role that required more listening than speaking. I was not the expert, my

CT was. I wanted to talk many times but bit my tongue because I knew my job was to listen. (TC 57)

When it was time to teach rather than just observe, our teacher candidates found that listening required other personal characteristics and skills associated with problem solving and multitasking:

During my field I learned that listening is a very powerful tool. You need to listen to staff and most importantly the student. [This is] very valuable in [dealing with] discipline problems; listen and figure out the best solution. (TC 52)

I thought that listening would be very easy but realized it is hard to give 100% attention while trying to concentrate on what to ask next or cover next. (TC 14)

In the field I feel as though I am listening intently to the students, but I feel as though because of time it is hard for me to allow all the students to speak and for me to concentrate fully on what they are saying when I have to also be thinking about what to discuss next. (TC 3)

Today my listening skills were challenged. I didn't realize how tough it is to listen to the many things students want to say while trying to conduct a class. As I listened, I needed to also observe the class. This was a new task for me. (TC 7)

One teacher candidate recognized the broader array of components associated with the art of listening, saying, "I will continue to listen openly. Even to my students' faces. Yes, faces speak even when their mouths are silent." We were impressed with the extent to which this candidate was attuned to the nonverbal cues of listening.

At the end of the field experience our teacher candidates wrote entries documenting thoughts about their present listening as well as considering future implications:

I am going to say listening [is the skill that needs improvement] because it is the most overlooked of the communication skills, but also the most important. I personally believe a teacher can never be too good of a listener. There are virtually unlimited settings, situations, and opportunities for teachers to listen. I have never denied how much I like to talk, but it is not to suggest I have no idea how important it is to listen. I will continue to monitor how I do in this disposition. (TC 8)

I found that much of the focus of my listening entries changed from my own merits as a listener, to deficiencies I had in listening. It seems that it is easier to pinpoint and critique myself on this topic when I am the central figure of the class. I think this transformation from student to teacher was quite evident in the continued realization that I have much to work on in the area of listening and how it relates to re-phrasing and questioning. (TC 63)

This seems to be one of the few teacher dispositions where our teacher candidates actually started projecting into the future. Respect, on the other hand, remained solidly grounded in the present.

RESPECT

Some teacher candidates discovered that the disposition of *respect* acquired new descriptors in the context of the K–12 classroom. They came to understand and identify with respect as an act of reciprocity within the university classroom. This understanding led to the expectation that if they respected someone it would automatically be returned (refer to chapter 3). They were surprised that this was not the case in the public school setting.

As the semester has progressed, and I have come to learn more about teaching, this area [respect] of the PQI holds a different meaning than it did at the beginning of the semester. (TC 14)

This role of respect has flip-flopped. In the classroom, I was the one giving the respect [to the teacher] and in field experience, I was the teacher getting the respect [maybe]. It was a hard transition to get used to. (TC 75)

The teacher candidates noted that respect was an essential compo-
nent to classroom management:

> Respect can be a hard thing to gain in a classroom if you don't act in
> control or fill the authority figure . . . have to have a definite notice-
> able presence in the room. (TC 68)

> Today a young man called another student a "fag." I talked to this
> young man politely about the meaning of this term and how it was not
> an appropriate form of language. . . . I feel that I am now able to con-
> trol my inner rage and deal with a situation like this one in a respect-
> ful manner. (TC 12)

Reducing sarcasm and bullying required a classroom structure that
honored, promoted, and ensured respect. Teacher candidates also
desired connectedness with their students so that they could "en-
joy" the profession and positively affect student learning. Many of
them worked diligently to build mutual respect within their classrooms:

> It amazes me the lack of respect some students have for their teachers.
> Is this a new thing? I don't remember school being this way. (TC 78)

> Today I led a class discussion and I discovered how hard it can be at
> times to show consideration to all students' ideas. Even when stu-
> dents' ideas seem off-base, you still have to consider their ideas with
> an open mind. (TC 8)

> Being in the field taught me that I need to respect a student's right to
> choose not to perform in school. Once I have tried everything I can
> possibly do . . . that's all I can do. (TC 54)

Yet another teacher candidate recognized the close ties between respect, relationships, and classroom management:

> Building personal relationships on a firm foundation of respect has
> proven very beneficial in reducing some of the classroom manage-

ment issues that were present in the first few weeks. Showing even difficult students strong respect makes it more difficult for some of them to disrespect me, I have found. (TC 55)

At times there was evidence of significant growth in a teacher candidate's ability to recognize and write about their experience with a particular disposition that spanned from the university classroom to the clinical field classroom and back again. For example, in this category, one teacher candidate started the semester using the very language that we provided in our descriptors, writing, "Showed due courtesy and consideration for group members while they were speaking." A middle-of-the-semester entry moved to "Showed respect for a classmate when he brought up negative points or argued with our group by not engaging in the argument and listening to my classmate's points before responding, so as to maintain group unity and cooperation." Toward the end of the field experience, the same teacher candidate wrote,

> Showing respect for myself has been most difficult. . . . I am still learning how to function as a teacher and a person at the same time. I dislike having to constantly chastise students for their language and behavior; thus, I often let certain comments or actions directed at me go without addressing them. I would rather ignore the misbehavior and move on . . . however, they [the K–12 students] expect to be chastised and threatened . . . so, finding my own balance of respect for myself and respect for other students has been very challenging. (TC 64)

Overall, the number and scope of the entries that teacher candidates wrote on respect in the K–12 setting were minimal and narrow (focus was on self and students). When it came to addressing professionalism in this same context, the number of entries increased exponentially. In addition, the focus was primarily inward, with only tangential regard for students and some mention of cooperating teachers.

PROFESSIONALISM

While in our university classrooms, teacher candidates' entries regarding *professionalism* in their PQIs were mainly about accepting positive criticism and feedback from peers and university professors. Our teacher candidates were in the early stages of role transition from student-learner to teacher-learner, so it was difficult for them to apply the descriptors of professionalism in the PQI to this emerging teacher identity. They were still responding to their perceptions of the power structure or hierarchy that they were accustomed to in a university classroom.

Once they started their field experiences the teacher candidates came face-to-face with the complex dynamics of professionalism as experienced by teachers. They encountered issues such as, What is professionalism really, other than acting right? Will I know it if I see it or don't see it? What impact will it have on me as I try to acquire it?

A majority of the teacher candidates associated appearance, timeliness, and preparedness with this disposition. These highly visible aspects of professionalism are epitomized in the following entries:

> I found the kids judged me by how I looked and acted. . . . I didn't have the luxury of having time to get to know them. Each day I had to put on my professional look. (TC 57)

> While [in the classroom], I had to be professional every day. It was important to keep a professional rapport while interacting with my students. I made sure I did not wear jeans, I did my hair, and was on time every day. . . . It was a shocker! (TC 50)

> My biggest concern was how close in age I am to the students, and if they would see me as a teacher figure. I dress appropriately to assist my professionalism and to show I am serious about my job. I monitor my body positions to also portray myself as a confident individual. (TC 9)

> In the field, I always made sure to dress and act appropriately, as well as be on time and prepared. I think that this is a big part of being and acting like a professional. (TC 34)

> Even though I am only a few years older than the students, they took me seriously because of my choice of vocabulary, attire, and preparedness. (TC 42)

> I saw professionalism every day in some way, shape, or form. Just the way of interacting with everyone and still holding yourself to that higher standard and being prepared . . . (TC 61)

Some teacher candidates were seemingly awed as they continued to develop their teacher identity—moving further away from the role of college student:

> I did not think students would think of me [as a professional]. . . . The first day that a student called me Mr./s._____ and they all quieted down to listen to me speak, a weird feeling came over me. . . . I can do this. I can interact with students and other teachers in a very professional manner without feeling awkward. (TC 20)

> There were a few instances where I did not handle student behavioral issues very professionally. Sometimes I tended to act somewhat as a student myself when dealing with these issues. (TC 16)

We smiled and cheered as we observed what we believe to be a natural progression, because teacher candidates often see it as an epiphany. Yet another teacher candidate found overlap between an emerging role as a teacher and an existing role as a parent:

> I was amazed at how I fell into a professional role. Perhaps being a parent as well as my previous jobs helped me to handle the many questions and tasks I needed to handle at one time—multitasking. (TC 41)

On a different note, some teacher candidates had experiences where students tried to promote a friendship and blur the line between teacher and student. They felt that their identity as a teacher was threatened and emphasized to the students that they were professional teachers who should be respected in that role. As one teacher candidate put it, "I worked on making my boundaries clear." Also, the desire to bring humor into the classroom and remain professional was a tightrope for some:

> I am having fun with the students today, laughing and joking. I hope I'm not appearing unprofessional! I don't think so, because I feel I am connecting with the students in a positive way. (TC 13)

> Now that I have gotten to know the students better, I feel myself acting like them. I do catch myself and remember that I do need to be more professional . . . good to joke around if it is appropriate. (TC 65)

These teacher candidates seem unwilling to buy into the advice "Don't smile until Christmas," but are ill equipped to be professionally casual with their students. There is no guarantee that they will gain insights through their field experience into the subtleties surrounding interpersonal relationships in the K–12 environment.

Public schools are staffed by a variety of teachers—highly competent, outright incompetent, and every conceivable combination in between. When teacher candidates enter the classroom, there is no assurance as to where their cooperating teacher will fall on this continuum:

> It is difficult to maintain a professional attitude and disposition when faculty and staff have given up trying to maintain [them] . . . although it shouldn't have. This affected my professionalism as I adopted the same discussion patterns of talking about students or faculty even when other students were present. (TC 64)

> I find it odd, but not wrong, that my dress for classes is much more formal than my cooperating teacher's . . . [also that] teachers tend to be cynical around each other. (TC 73)

> There were some interesting, though not surprising, moments when I noticed deficiencies in the professionalism of some "professional"

teachers. I was disappointed at times, but I know many of them attribute it to "burnout." (TC 63)

Observed teachers while working together determining students' placements and scheduling for the next year. . . . I never heard anyone raise their voice or utter an unkind word. Their problem-solving strategies taught me much about professionalism. (TC 49)

Our years of experience in a variety of educational contexts instilled in us an understanding of and appreciation for the complexities of teaching. We work diligently in our university courses to convey this sentiment to our teacher candidates. Our teacher candidates' reactions to their cooperating teachers varied from judgment, to empathy, to praise. We were pleased that they were willing to allow human frailties to be exposed and able to consider how the teaching profession can wear at one's resilience.

We read some of the entries with smiles on our faces, joy in our hearts, and the sense of a milestone being achieved. For many, the connection between dispositions and teacher identity was becoming evident:

I have found that looking and acting professional in the field is extremely important in order to separate yourself from the learner. This is important for how you see yourself as well as for how faculty or staff and students see you. . . . I will have to change the way I shop for myself. (TC 78)

Being professional comes easy. I think it is because I'm really starting to love this profession. (TC 68)

Since this field experience, I have really begun to take note of how I act in public (like driving nicely) and maintaining what I feel a teacher should act like. It is an interesting feeling to become "a teacher." (TC 10)

I have grown into a teacher. I don't feel like a student any longer. (TC 8 and TC 1)

I want to be a role model more than ever before. (TC 21)

I seemed to have returned to [the university] class with a new perspective. Having been in the field, I'm much more attentive to what's happening during class. I ask myself, is this professionalism? (TC 53)

REFLECTION

Reflection is like self-assessment; it is difficult to do because you do not know if you are asking the appropriate questions or whether you should believe your answers. Reflection hangs in the air like an elusive snowflake in the winter breeze, always just a little out of reach. Our teacher candidates grappled with reflection and wrote entries that brought mind and emotion together. What also becomes apparent is the tight connection between reflection and the other teacher dispositions.

Teacher candidates' entries in their PQIs document a concern about their relationships with the cooperating teacher and students, as well as the effectiveness of their teaching and growth as a professional:

It was easy to say that I was accomplishing various aspects of my PQI while in class. Then again, I honestly believe that we can more or less fool ourselves into thinking we are behaving in certain ways. However, in the field, it is fairly obvious if we are meeting certain PQI goals based on the feedback we receive. (TC 71)

I could use more development on reflection. I believe it is a very important part of teaching and I think I could have taken more time to reflect on my teaching. (TC 1)

Our teacher candidates wanted to suspend initial judgments while working with their students, not relying on first impressions but striving to build reciprocal relationships that would enhance learning. Attention to this objective is evidenced by the following:

In working with adolescents, I think it is necessary that teachers do not judge the students from first impressions, as we have said in class. Students don't always show a teacher their full personality or real attitude. It was necessary to suspend my initial impressions until I got to know the students better. (TC 34)

This seems to be an area that I find myself working on every day. I try really hard to suspend initial judgments about students. In order to do this, I need to critique my attitudes and behaviors and today I found myself doing exactly that. (TC 8)

This vein of reflection naturally moved into the area of instruction:

I was always reflecting on my attitudes and behaviors in my field, trying to act mature and responsible. I needed to suspend any judgments I may have had about a student or teaching method until I saw it in action and it was successful/unsuccessful. (TC 62)

In the [field] classroom I was able to reflect on what I had learned in the [university] classroom and bring them together by incorporating them into my lessons and teaching. I feel that my reflecting on information that I had learned in the [university] classroom made me a more effective teacher and presenter. (TC 36)

The most reflection comes between classes when I have to consider what elements of the lesson need to be changed. . . . I have found that this is a strength of mine because the last hour is always better than the previous two from the amount of reflection and modification between classes. (TC 14)

Several candidates agreed that reflection was something a teacher did every day to stay sharp, "Every day is a reflection; therefore, we learn from our mistakes and keep on moving." Others acknowledged the human factor as well:

At times, I didn't like reflecting about what happened during the day. I felt reflection was hard because of the mood I was in. (TC 22)

Today was hard for me because I didn't have a very good attitude. I was very tired and I thought by the second class period I got myself into it. You have to do this as a teacher. The students will pick up on your information more if you are into the class. (TC 17)

I reflected today on my teaching activities . . . how I may have helped a student or confused another. This is all just mind-boggling, but all in a day's work. (TC 10)

RUMINATIONS

In many ways teacher dispositions took on a new life when teacher candidates entered K–12 classrooms. To a certain extent we expected this; however, we had no idea what shape it would take. Our teacher candidates learned that teacher dispositions are not static; when the context changed so did the application of the dispositions. Each disposition has a nature or essence that identifies it, but it is contextually influenced. When the context shifts, nurture takes over as the participants and the dynamics offer unique interactive opportunities. One of the key players in the K–12 context is the cooperating teacher.

Cooperating teachers are an integral part of the context within which teacher candidates develop their knowledge, skills, and dispositions. Their interactions impact teacher candidates' perspectives of the mentoring process and its role in their growth and development as professionals. The dichotomy that can exist is supported by the voices of these two teacher candidates:

My CT seems to wing a lot of the lesson. I'm not happy about this. . . . I felt like a burden to my CT. I felt like I was more work for him. He did not do much mentoring. I wish I had a CT that would take me under his or her wing. (TC 66)

Having an hour each way, I found myself reflecting on each day during my commute . . . questioning methods and content. . . . CT would listen to my questions daily . . . looked forward to this. . . . I will be quick to find someone at my school to confide in, as I will want to share my ideas with others. (TC 70)

We can hear the disappointment and the crying out for a mentor from the first candidate and the confirmation of a supportive experience for the second candidate. They will both carry the desire for collegiality into their careers. Regardless, most of our candidates agree with the following declaration: "This whole experience was the single most important or best experience that I have had thus far. It reinforced to me that I made the correct career choice."

The field experience confirmed for many teacher candidates their career choice. Here again, the power associated with the field experience reaffirmed our commitment to acknowledge and include cooperating teachers in the broader spectrum of the teacher education program. Traditionally, cooperating teachers worked with professional knowledge and skills. We contend that they should also be involved with the third portion of the teacher education triad—dispositions. Acting on this premise, we sought out our cooperating teachers' beliefs and insights about teacher dispositions. In the next chapter, we share these beliefs and insights, their congruence with our teacher education program, and the potential effect they have on teacher candidates' emerging teacher identities.

Chapter Five

What Do Cooperating Teachers See?

The school year was well under way when Chris got word from the university that another set of teacher candidates was coming to the building for a six-week clinical experience. This information sparked the following initial thoughts: *Wow, it hardly seems possible that I've been at this for 15 years. I bet I've worked with six to eight teacher candidates during that time. I wonder if I should volunteer to have someone in my classroom this fall?*

Chris is concerned about the university's request that cooperating teachers spend more time talking with these teacher candidates about matters beyond content and strategies. The internal dialogue begins: *I don't ever remember talking with my cooperating teachers about how respect plays out in the classroom, how to promote active listening or the type of collaborative opportunities teachers have during the school year. In fact, I don't think the phrase* teacher dispositions *ever came up. You were either good with kids or you weren't. You either got along with your peers or you didn't. No one really put these ideas into words. But now that I think about it, I always knew who really made a connection with students and wondered just how they did it. Maybe if I'd had practiced analyzing this more affective aspect of teaching, I could have incorporated specific elements*

Authors' note: We would like to thank John Hoover for his insights and encouragement.

into my teacher identity in a more deliberate way than the trial-and-error method I used.

Who am I kidding? There isn't time during the school day for conversations about teacher dispositions to take place. We have 4-minute passing periods between classes and I'm expected to monitor the halls. There are at least 300 more students in the building than can comfortably fit, so the commotion and noise level in the halls doesn't really lend itself to critical reflection. Where in my day am I supposed to carve out time for these critical conversations? I don't think I'm up to the challenge of a teacher candidate this year.

Chris is torn between the potential time commitment and the possible educational benefits that accompany working with teacher candidates. The internal discourse continues: *The last few teacher candidates I worked with were really up-to-date on the content. The books they recommended I read were truly beneficial as I thought about reorganizing my curriculum. And the insights they had about multiple intelligences and working with English language learners couldn't have come at a more appropriate time. I don't think they recognized the usefulness of that information, but when I looked out on the growing diversity among my students, I found immediate application. Not only did I benefit, but my students also seemed to benefit from the presence of these enthusiastic future teachers.*

It's amazing how much more teacherly attention students get—when I think about how many more students I have in class this year compared to 3 years ago, it's a wonder I can remember their names, let alone meet their individual learning needs. Maybe I will volunteer my time and classroom space again this semester.

Do you know what thoughts and concerns go through your cooperating teachers' minds as they decide whether to mentor your teacher candidates? How might you find out? And what will you do with the information once you have it?

Education programs have a longstanding tradition whereby they rely on the combined efforts of teacher educators and inservice (cooperating) teachers to prepare future generations of teachers. Teacher educators are often thought to be responsible for theory while cooperating teachers are responsible for practice. That is, teacher educators work with teacher candidates to develop knowledge of content and pedagogy; cooperating teachers provide a safe place for them to use this knowledge with students. This traditional structure establishes an idiosyncratic educational triangle — that being the relationship between teacher educators, cooperating teachers, and teacher candidates. The person who we believe is in the most precarious position within this triangle is the teacher candidate.

Teacher candidates find themselves moving between two worlds (i.e., the university and K–12 classrooms) within which they endeavor to combine theory and practice. As we examine these two worlds, we recognize some tensions that come from the fact that these worlds are often disparate. Legend has it that theory exists only on college and university campuses and is of no use in K–12 classrooms. K–12 classrooms are considered the "real world," implying that teacher education courses exist in a "fake world."

There is also a hierarchical structure to education to which is attached a teacher's perceived value. High school teaching is more prestigious than middle and elementary school teaching. College teaching is even more prestigious. In addition, this hierarchy sets the stage for placing blame when students do not have the perceived requisite knowledge for a particular grade. College teachers blame the K–12 schools for not teaching students the basics, high school teachers blame the middle school teachers, and so forth.

The sentiments associated with "real" and "fake" worlds, teachers' perceived value, and the blame game can perpetuate an us-against-them mentality within the triangular relationships of teacher education. As such, those people involved seem incapable of recognizing that we are all players in the same play. Our unity of purpose may be to promote an environment conducive to the growth and development of knowledge, skills, and dispositions among all three players—reciprocity within a three-dimensional forum—to enhance teaching and learning.

Our most recent endeavor pertaining to this notion of three-dimensional reciprocity involves our work with teacher dispositions. As illustrated throughout this book, we spend a great deal of time and energy addressing teacher dispositions with our secondary teacher candidates. Given that the context of our teacher education program includes substantive field experiences, we set out to discover cooperating teachers' perceptions regarding the teacher dispositions we promote.

Cooperating teachers play a vital role in the preparation of future teachers. For a variety of reasons, they open their classrooms to teacher candidates. Some feel a sense of professional responsibility to mentor and to nurture the next generation of teachers. Others anticipate "time off" from the day-to-day school routine. Still others are excited for the opportunity to learn new strategies from teacher candidates. Rarely, if ever, do they volunteer in anticipation of a financial windfall.

During any given field experience, cooperating teachers share their professional experiences with teacher candidates. Those most often shared revolve around strategies for instruction as well as classroom management—both of which are skills based. At times, these insights are encouraging and hopeful, with a healthy dose of realism. At other times, the insights are discouraging and daunting, with an abundance of cynicism.

Cooperating teachers tend to assume that teacher candidates will come to their classrooms with an adequate knowledge base and take the initiative to identify and address any gaps in it. The concept of teacher dispositions receives inadvertent attention; comments most commonly refer to whether the teacher candidate is a nice person and/or gets along with the kids. Regardless of the content and/or tenor of the cooperating teachers' insights, the time teacher candidates spend in these classrooms is often touted by them as the most influential portion of their teacher education program. We, as teacher educators, are concerned that this influence be productive.

To date, the powerful voices of cooperating teachers appear to be at best, underrepresented, at worst, missing from the growing dialogue on teacher dispositions. Cooperating teachers' perceptions can add depth to current conversations surrounding this element of the knowledge–skills–dispositions triangle. Their perceptions also influence the environment within which our teacher candidates further explore and develop their teacher identities, which are grounded in their knowledge, skills, and dispositions. We designed a survey to determine if our chosen teacher dispositions resonated with the cooperating teachers who participate in our clinical field experiences (see appendixes 7 and 8).

By soliciting these perceptions, we intend to identify connections and misconnections between the contexts of our university classrooms and K–12 classrooms with respect to our identified teacher dispositions. Another goal is to include the perspectives of cooperating teachers in our university classroom context in order to enhance our ability to "make these dispositions real and demonstrable to preservice teachers" (Powers, 1999, p. 3). Still another goal is to prepare teacher candidates to work productively within K–12 contexts whether or not they support the teacher dispositions we espouse in our university courses.

As you continue to read our views on the survey process, the views of our cooperating teachers, and our interpretation of these views, we hope to spark ideas to enable you to address teacher dispositions within the context of your teacher education programs.

OUR APPREHENSIVE VIEWS

The week after we mailed out our surveys to cooperating teachers, we attended and presented at a national symposium on teacher dispositions. In our presentation, we shared our survey, goals, and potential contributions to the dialogue on teacher dispositions with colleagues from other teacher education programs. The overwhelming opinion of our college and university colleagues was that our survey would not garner any new insights regarding teacher dispositions. That is, they could not envision anyone who would mark anything other than "Agree" to each of our 24 survey items. Their suggestions focused on recrafting the opening stem ("Teachers should . . .") in such a way as to determine whether cooperating teachers were actually doing these things in their professional practice (e.g., "I currently . . .").

Needless to say, we became apprehensive over the potential of our survey. The surveys were in the mail, and we heard voices that suggested it was all for naught. We dwelled on and then sorted through the comments over dinner and the long plane ride home. We realized that during the development process, we actually contemplated whether to structure our survey in a more global or more personal way. We opted for a more global structure because we did not want to appear to be standing in judgment of our cooperating teachers.

Public classrooms and teachers receive heavy scrutiny from the outside; we did not want to perpetuate that sentiment unnecessarily. Those responding to our survey would do so without the benefit of us being there to reinforce the intended collegial tone and to clarify any potential misperceptions. In addition, we believed that a more global structure for the survey would support our initial goal of determining whether there was public school recognition of the teacher dispositions we espoused with our teacher candidates. Our thought was, if we reach some agreement on the broader ideals regarding teacher dispositions, we could then use these insights to further investigate how these ideals are put into practice.

Thus, we regained some confidence in our survey structure ("Teachers should . . ."). By the time our plane landed, we reached two tentative conclusions. First, we could not take back the surveys; regardless of our apprehensions, cooperating teachers were receiving and hopefully responding to our survey. Second, you don't know if you don't go; we would determine our next move based on whatever insights the surveys uncovered.

COOPERATING TEACHERS' VIEWS
AND HOW WE INTERPRET THEM

As with most survey research, our surveys straggled in one at a time. We grew concerned that maybe our cooperating teachers were uninterested or too busy to respond. Fortunately, this was not the case. In the end, 57.4% of our cooperating teachers shared their insights on the teacher dispositions that we use with our teacher candidates. Table 1 shows that in all but one instance, more than 90% of the cooperating teachers "agree" or "agree in part" with the survey items presented.

Table 1. Cooperating Teacher Survey Items in Descending Order by Percentage of "Agree" Responses

The teacher should . . .	% Agree	% Agree + Agree in Part	Mean	SD
10. communicate effectively with students, parents, and colleagues	95.9	100.0	4.96	0.20
8. create connections to subject matter that are meaningful or relevant to students	92.6	99.2	4.91	0.36
4. be thoughtful and responsive listeners	91.8	100.0	4.92	0.28
23. communicate in ways that demonstrate respect for feelings, ideas, and contributions of others	90.0	98.4	4.90	0.30
12. use a variety of instructional strategies to optimize student learning	89.3	100.0	4.89	0.31
19. treat students with dignity and respect at all times	88.5	99.2	4.87	0.41
21. be patient when working with students	87.7	99.2	4.87	0.36
20. be willing to receive feedback and assessment of their teaching	84.4	99.2	4.84	0.39
1. be committed to critical reflection for professional growth	83.5	99.2	4.83	0.40
15. have high expectations for all students and help them achieve these	81.1	99.2	4.79	0.52
18. be sensitive to student differences	81.0	96.7	4.75	0.60

(continued)

Table 1. (*continued*)

The teacher should . . .	% Agree	% Agree + Agree in Part	Mean	SD
24. seriously consider the quality of their responses or reactions to situations and feedback from students, colleagues, parents, etc.	80.7	99.2	4.79	0.47
22. be open to adjusting and revising plans to meet student needs	77.0	98.4	4.75	0.51
6. engage in discussions about new ideas in the teaching profession	74.6	98.4	4.73	0.48
14. assume responsibility when working with others	74.6	94.3	4.68	0.61
13. stay current with the evolving nature of the teaching profession	73.8	99.2	4.73	0.46
16. view teaching as a collaborative effort among educators	73.6	98.3	4.71	0.52
9. listen to colleagues' ideas and suggestions to improve instruction	73.0	100	4.73	0.45
17. understand students have certain needs that must be met before learning can take place	72.7	98.3	4.70	0.53
11. work well with others in implementing a common curriculum	68.6	95.0	4.60	0.69
3. actively seek out professional growth opportunities	66.9	97.5	4.63	0.59
5. demonstrate and encourage democratic interaction in the classroom and school	58.7	88.4	4.41	0.85
2. cooperate with colleagues in planning instruction	58.2	98.4	4.56	0.56
7. engage in research-based teaching practices	28.7	91.8	4.16	0.72

The fact that cooperating teachers' responses are negatively skewed provides content validity for the dispositions represented in our survey. That is, the various teacher dispositions that we culled from research literature, personal public-school experiences, existing education programs, and standards from accrediting agencies are recognized as important by many cooperating teachers in public schools who work with our secondary teacher candidates. What we do not know is whether our list is perceived as all-inclusive or if there is any perceived order of importance.

This high response rate seems to support the comments provided by our colleagues at the teacher disposition conference. In fact, three cooperating teachers wrote general comments at the end of the survey such as "Who would not agree?" Worth noting, however, is that their suggestions for recrafting the survey were quite different from our colleagues in higher education. These cooperating teachers each focused on time as the primary, broad-sweeping constraint placed upon teachers that should be considered. As one cooperating teacher offered, "The statements should not be 'Teachers should . . .,' but 'As a teacher, do you realistically have time to . . .?'" In addition to the general comments made by these three cooperating teachers, ten others made at least one comment on their survey specifically regarding time constraints.

Time is truly a factor that influences every decision made within K–16 education, and everyone's time is valuable. However, time is structured quite differently in the K–12 context than in the college or university context. Sometimes teacher educators forget the different time constraints faced by our cooperating teachers.

As we think about the relationships within the triangle of teacher educators, cooperating teachers, and teacher candidates, there needs to be clearer understanding and appreciation of the concept of time and how time manifests itself differently within these two contexts. We suggest this not as an excuse for why innovation and change cannot happen, but as an explanation for why innovation and change look different or may *need* to look different in these two worlds. We catch ourselves wondering (thankfully, less and less), why cooperating teachers cannot better accommodate our teacher candidates' needs for shared reflection on classroom experiences.

Many narrative comments included in the surveys reminded us that there is little wiggle-room in a K–12 school day. Cooperating teachers must find little moments sprinkled throughout the day to address multiple issues, including the mentoring of our teacher candidates. Thus, any gulf between what cooperating teachers believe they *should* do and what they *actually* do may be mitigated by the time constraints placed upon them by sources beyond their control.

This concept of time surfaced in narrative comments throughout cooperating teachers' surveys, suggesting that time is an influential factor associated with multiple teacher dispositions. Nuances such as these manifest themselves when we look beyond the content validity of the teacher dispositions identified on the basis of our survey results. While we are pleased with the content validity, we are intrigued by the subtle differences in perceptions that became evident when we examined the survey items from the viewpoint of the percentage of cooperating teachers who marked "Agree" only.

The four survey items listed in the Agree column of table 1 that accrued greater than 90% agreement represent our teacher dispositions *listening* (questions 4 and 10; 2/3), *reflection* (question 8; 1/5), and *respect* (question 23; 1/4). A common element among these four questions seems to be the communication processes that exist within the public school setting, with students taking center stage. As our respondents thought about their worlds of teaching, the ability to listen, to reflect on how best to communicate content and to do so clearly and sensitively were foremost in their minds.

While elements of listening and respect appeared valued, survey items associated with these two dispositions received the fewest number of narrative comments from cooperating teachers. Our teacher candidates also wrote the fewest number of comments in their *personal qualitative inventory* (PQI) regarding these two dispositions while they were in their secondary block courses. In addition, the nature of the comments that were made by both cooperating teachers and teacher candidates suggests a casual attention to these dispositions within known environments. Familiarity can foster complacency.

Familiarity also provides fertile ground for the assumptions that surface in both teacher education courses and K–12 classrooms. As a result, we may not actually know the characteristics of listening and respect when they are present or when they are absent. In addition, we may not even understand the consequences of their presence or absence because we are too close to those things to see clearly.

Cooperating teachers rarely have the time or opportunity to examine their assumptions under new light as our teacher candidates did when they entered the K–12 classrooms. It may be that teachers at all levels need help making the familiar strange in order to systematically and intentionally (re-)examine, nurture, and (re-)develop these and other dispositions that promote a positive and effective teaching and learning environment, thus promoting three-dimensional reciprocity.

Further exploration of the Agree column of table 1 reveals that each of the four questions associated with *cooperation and collaboration* (questions 2, 5, 11, and 14) fell below 75%, with questions 2 and 5 falling below 60%. In addition to the relatively low percentage of support, cooperation and collaboration garnered the most narrative comments (53 total) across the four questions pertaining to this disposition. And question 2 received the most narrative comments for a single survey item (18 from 18 different cooperating teachers).

We think it bears mentioning that questions 2, 11, and 14 focus more on cooperation and collaboration among teachers; question 5 focuses more on cooperation and collaboration among teachers and students. Cooperating teachers seemed compelled to qualify their rankings about the role of cooperation and collaboration in education.

Obviously, some of our cooperating teachers recognize the importance of cooperation and collaboration with their peers as it serves to promote teaching and learning. However, only 2 of the 18 comments associated with question 2 specifically supported *cooperating with colleagues to plan instruction*, for example, "team work is always better than individual." The remainder of the cooperating teachers raised doubts about the practical application of this teacher disposition.

One cooperating teacher offered reservations that "as the only teacher of my subject area in my building it would not be productive." This sentiment implies that cooperation and collaboration is useful only when addressing issues within a content area. Such a reaction ignores the power of interdisciplinary curriculum as well as the benefits to teaching and learning that arise from examining students' learning and motivation from a cross-curricular perspective (see Martinello & Cook, 2000; Roberts & Kellough, 2000; Wood, 2005).

Time reemerges as a factor in relation to cooperation and collaboration. One cooperating teacher added the caveat "if given time during the work day," a second commented that "based on the time constraints this is not possible," and a third mentioned that "no time is allowed for this." These comments seem to support the assertion that teachers work in imposed isolation, that is, the school structure precludes working with others.

Additional conditions attached to cooperation and collaboration like the following statements from specific cooperating teachers (CTs) were also prevalent:

Teachers also need the freedom to teach in their own way. (CT 5)

Teachers have to work individually and use their unique teaching styles. (CT 29)

As long as that doesn't mean always accepting the lowest common denominator of quality and professionalism. (CT 31)

These narrative responses suggest that teachers may choose to work in isolation from a need to maintain some autonomy and/or a need to maintain some professional control over curriculum and instructional strategies. One cooperating teacher sums up the complexity of this disposition by saying, "The irony, at least at the secondary level, is that we profess to teach cooperation but seldom practice it."

We expected cooperating teachers' comments relating to imposed isolation to be a result of school structure and the impact it has on cooperation and collaboration. What we did not expect and find more worrisome is the notion of chosen isolation. An emerging theme among our cooperating teachers' comments is that they would choose to work alone even if given the time to work with others. This is troubling to us because we have first-hand experience with the rejuvenating and confirming power of cooperation and collaboration. Also, there is sufficient evidence to suggest that isolation among educators contributes to teacher attrition (see Certo & Fox, 2002; Darling-Hammond & Sclan, 1996; Feiman-Nemser, 2001). Cooperation and collaboration are also effective strategies to use with students in the teaching and learning environment (see Johnson, Johnson, & Holubec, 1998; Kauchak & Eggen, 2003; Ryder & Graves, 2003).

Our survey Question 5 ("Teachers should demonstrate and encourage democratic interaction in the classroom and school") brings K–12 students into the arena of cooperation and collaboration. As you will recall, this question received an Agree response rate of 58.7%. Of the nine cooperating teachers who wrote comments in conjunction with this question, the most supportive comments echoed this tone: "in some things but not in everything."

Two cooperating teachers seemed strongly opposed to this idea, as exemplified in the following comments: "My classroom is not a democracy. We would never get anything done if it were" and "The teacher should have complete control in the classroom—it is NOT a democracy! (Neither is the school)." The lack of endorsement for democratic interactions seems to run contrary to the longstanding emphasis placed on democracy in education (see Dewey, 1944; Engle & Ochoa, 1988; Parker, 2002). As presented, these data on cooperation and collaboration point to potential misconnections between what we espouse in our education courses, what educational researchers constitute as crucial to quality teaching, and what our cooperating teachers describe as important within their professional contexts.

The other teacher disposition that received only marginal support is *continuous learning*. Each of the four questions associated with this disposition (Questions 3, 6, 7, and 13) received less than a 75% Agree rating. This result is a bit discouraging as we contemplate the emphasis we place on helping K–12 students become lifelong learners. Seven cooperating teachers offered comments that endorsed this teacher disposition; one suggested that "a complacent teacher is a dead one," and another was convinced they "always can learn a new approach."

However, 20 cooperating teachers noted challenges involved with staying current on content and pedagogy. Time and money appear to be the most noted constraints in these areas. One cooperating teacher suggested that "missed time in class often makes training unattractive," while another noted that "[professional development] can get very expensive." Support from their districts was also a concern; a third cooperating teacher pointed out that engaging in discussions about new ideas in teaching "is often fruitless because of a lack of time or commitment by the school district." Still others asserted the following:

> In 35 years, I've seen things I tried and discarded many years ago return as today's "new ideas." (CT 54)

> What's new? (CT 11)

> Sometimes we have too many trends that come and go. (CT 27)

Here, time constraints were combined with agitation over the ever-present educational pendulum, something that did not surprise us. It seems natural that time would come together with the ebb and flow of educational trends. Teachers do not look favorably on time engaged in continuous learning when it involves what they perceive as old things with new names—a fact that rings loud and clear in their reactions to the query on research-based teaching practices.

Question 7 ("Teachers should engage in research-based teaching practices") received not only the lowest Agree response rate (28.7%) of the 24 survey items, but also the fewest supportive comments. In fact, there was no strong support for this item beyond being "aware of best practices," which we consider a bit different from the actual statement. Most cooperating teachers were willing to support this notion "only if they improve upon what is already being done" or if "this fits the curriculum and the teacher's own style."

Some cooperating teachers were concerned that "too often research-based teaching practices are so much the focus that what is natural to the teacher is lost." Others suggested that "replacing what works with something new that does not work is not a good practice." Yet another cooperating teacher lamented, "How do you get the research out to a group that is overworked and underpaid?"

As teacher researchers, we find the reaction to this specific item disconcerting. It could exemplify a belief in the ivory tower of academe or an attitude built on a lack of appreciation for the work of classroom teachers. This response also gives us cause to contemplate cooperating teachers' understanding of the concept "research-based teaching practices." Given our work as and with classroom teachers, we are inclined to believe that the cause lies in some combination of these and other factors as yet unidentified.

RUMINATIONS

Each and every educator has a teacher identity constructed from his or her knowledge, skills, and dispositions. This teacher identity can be consciously and unconsciously supported throughout a career. Teachers in K–12 classrooms often get wrapped up in and overwhelmed by curriculum standards, classroom management, and all the manifestations of the actions due to teachers and students coming together.

Given the competing demands of the profession, teachers may feel that they have no time or energy left to contemplate their teacher identities. If they do have time or energy, they tend to focus on those elements associated with their knowledge and skills and ignore their dispositions. This neglect can reduce the capacity to reflect on the role that our human qualities and commitments play in energizing our creativity and resiliency as we plan curriculum and instruction.

Our teacher candidates, on the other hand, spend at least 10 weeks consciously examining their dispositions as well as their knowledge and skills, and pondering the potential influence of this triad on teaching and learning in the K–12 environment. As they anticipate working in the classroom, teacher candidates think about how the integration of their knowledge, skills, and dispositions might work best with their new students in a specific classroom context.

In all too many instances, cooperating teachers drown out a teacher candidate's consideration of teacher identity by insisting that the teaching and learning environment be structured in a specific way, regardless of the impact on student learning. Other cooperating teachers even suggest that teacher candidates forget everything they learned in their teacher education courses in order to succeed in the classroom. As a result, success comes to be defined by traditionalism, which is focused on content knowledge and delivery.

We know from our survey that there is general support for the teacher dispositions we emphasize with our teacher candidates. Even so, we recognize that we do not have a conduit in place to tell cooperating teachers what we are actually doing with dispositions and why we are doing it. We need to create a process to further develop mutually agreed upon teacher dispositions. Next, we need to identify, validate, and reconcile diverse perspectives on additional teacher dispositions. Until such a procedure is in place, we cannot create a supportive environment in which teacher candidates can explore their teacher dispositions in the K–12 classroom. Our final reflections in chapter 6 address numerous questions such as this.

Chapter Six

What Do We See Looking Backward? Looking Forward?

As our story winds down (before gearing up again), we are reminded that our teacher educators chose to travel the raucous road of intrigue surrounding the affective world of teacher dispositions. They immersed themselves in the recursive process of living, implementing, and assessing these dispositions. Our teacher educators are convinced that the time spent and the investigations done offer their own rewards. They had the opportunity to model the dynamic nature of teacher dispositions. Their goal was to help teacher candidates recognize and reflect on the manifestations of their own personal attributes in the public classroom environment. Did they succeed? To date, our teacher educators feel gratified with the outcomes—a raised consciousness and a newfound commitment to teacher dispositions. However, they recognize that this is an ongoing journey. Where might it take them? Is this where you would go?

LOOKING BACKWARD

Education, by its very nature, is results-oriented. Today, such results seem fixated on accountability through assessment—worth must be proven. We recognize that there are standardized ways of assessing knowledge and skills, for example, the Praxis tests for content and pedagogy (Educational Testing Services). However, until recently, the assessment of dispositions was left to happenstance or ignored altogether.

Our intent was not to come up with a standardized way to identify or evaluate teacher dispositions. *Personal qualitative inventory* (PQI), the very title of our product, signifies our shift away from a standardized view. That is, we moved from thinking about them as traits that others evaluate to thinking about them as attributes that individuals inventory, explore, and examine in consert with others.

Throughout each semester, we offer written and oral feedback to teacher candidates on the basis of the messages they write in their PQIs. Do we need to compliment them? Is it enough to say "this is wonderful"? What kind of reinforcement might they need from us? We ponder our feedback because it is the process we use to bolster teacher candidates' confidence in their reflective endeavors, which in turn, supports one of our goals—raising the consciousness of being a lifelong reflective practitioner regarding their dispositions as well as their knowledge and skills. We believe that if teacher candidates develop this as a habit of mind, they will maintain it as an integral part of their teacher identity.

While possibly naive, another goal is to encourage teacher candidates to practically think about what is in their minds and souls with respect to teacher dispositions. The PQI provides an appropriate space to record this thinking; thinking that we believe is rather powerful for our teacher candidates. One teacher candidate used this space to evaluate a longstanding belief regarding the role of teacher talk in the classroom:

> Teachers like to talk and I'm no exception. . . . I've been trying to listen more and speak less. This is hard, but I am making progress. This is interesting because students often look to teachers as "the source" of information. (TC 48)

But how can teachers be a source of information and be quiet at the same time? What philosophical shift needs to occur to find some balance? There is a growing recognition for this teacher candidate that giving information needs to be integrated with the art of listening. The thought of honoring students' voices and considering the impact it might have on the teacher's role in the classroom is given an outlet through the PQI.

The PQI also provides a safe space for teacher candidates to struggle with the complexity of teacher dispositions. One teacher candidate struggled with multiple teacher dispositions vying for position to set the tone for an effective outcome.

> Listening is one of those things that seems to be a challenge for many people (true listening). I have always thought—as most of us do—of myself as an effective listener. I now find that I have an extremely hard time listening when the credibility of the person is diminished. My CT has been giving me some valid advice that I have a hard time listening to because I don't see him as a credible source. (TC 71)

Teacher candidates needed to deal with the disposition of respect in order to benefit from the valuable advice they heard. We consider this an example of dispositions doing battle with one another. This is a real situation that we all face at some point in our careers. How can we help teacher candidates recognize the importance of the process and encourage them to persevere while wrestling with often competing dispositions?

Yet another example of the power of the PQI is the honest introspection that it can provoke (this teacher candidate was in the fourth year of the teacher education program):

> This whole process has been a continuous learning experience. I find myself quite lacking in classroom management expertise—and I'm not even sure I want to develop the skills that would be necessary to improve in that area. Very confused. (TC 60)

The processes surrounding the PQI encourage teacher candidates to dig into the recesses of their minds and spirits, and identify their strengths and challenges. Teacher candidates cannot hide or ignore the issues revealed through the personal talk of the PQI. Once these issues are identified, the teacher candidates must address them in order to grow and develop as professionals.

The previous chapters described intricacies of working with teacher dispositions. We outlined the process we went through to identify teacher dispositions that resonated with the research on effective teaching and complemented our philosophies of teacher education as well as the context of our program. We walked you through the evolution of the process and product that we use to encourage teacher candidates to explore how teacher dispositions are manifested in their teacher identities over the course of a semester.

We also devoted two chapters to a plethora of teacher candidates' voices as they worked with dispositions, initially in our university courses and then in their individual K–12 field placements. Finally, we examined our cooperating teachers' perceptions in an effort to identify connections and/or misconnections between the contexts of our university classrooms and K–12 classrooms with respect to our identified teacher dispositions.

The fact that these perspectives reinforce the multifaceted nature of teacher dispositions both excites and exhausts us for the same reasons. This complexity requires us to be energetic and flexible with each new group of teacher candidates and cooperating teachers while remaining sincerely open to the individual needs that permeate these groups—what a stimulating yet fatiguing challenge! In this chapter, we discuss some of what we see in our future woven around a substantial number of questions that emerged.

LOOKING FORWARD

Our work with teacher candidates is ongoing—at least as long as we are employed! So, too, is our work with teacher dispositions. The more we worked with the perspectives represented in our data, the more we realized how many messages arise when people are asked to contemplate the affective domain and to then share their insights. We need to remember to revisit and contemplate these multiple messages to remind ourselves of the many ways people see things and how greatly influenced we all are by everything that communicates—body, mind, and voice.

As Palmer (1998) reminds us, "depth is depth." We cannot understand the depth of others until we understand our own depth. Reflection can reinforce the complexity of dispositions specifically and teaching in general. As teacher educators, we gained valuable insights through our initial work with teacher dispositions, including the realization that numerous questions remain. Through the recursive nature of our work, new questions emerged that inspire us to continue to grapple with *our* knowledge, skills, and dispositions.

When introducing dispositions (as well as knowledge and skills) to teacher candidates, it is important not to assume levels of understanding or agreement upon the definitions provided. Teacher candidates need to feel that their prior knowledge matches those with more experience. Differentiating between knowledge, skills, and dispositions through critical discussions validates what they bring to the table, helps them recognize how they know this, and reveals their misunderstandings and gaps regarding these concepts.

Teacher educators need to purposefully teach what dispositions are, for example, working through the various descriptors, providing concrete examples, and asking questions to stimulate critical thinking. We believe that the art of reflection lies somewhere within this process. Do teacher candidates independently recognize the cues and questions that can stimulate *their* reflection?

Introducing the concept of teacher dispositions to each new class also requires us to willingly make ourselves vulnerable. At the start of each semester, we need to prepare ourselves to greet a new set of teacher candidates who, as we know from past experiences, will be uncomfortable, uneasy, insecure, and possibly belligerent about the prospect of inventorying their dispositions. While they become accustomed to this new concept, we need to entertain their anger, frustration, and inquiry without personalizing it. This directly challenges *our* teacher dispositions, which allows us to act as models for the process.

We all tend to grow comfortable with in-depth conversations about teacher dispositions over the course of a semester. This comfort allows for frank and open discussions of the affective domain. At the end of the semester, teacher candidates are looking forward to further cultivating their dispositions in student teaching and beyond. We, on the other hand, retrace our steps and prepare to engage a new group of teacher candidates.

Can we demonstrate our ability and willingness to adjust to changing contexts in such a way as to help all fulfill their potential? How do we share relevant experiences of prior teacher candidates, without directing these novices in ways that are not theirs? We found that a different kind of dexterity is required from the professor as we strive to keep the notion of teacher dispositions complex, to avoid indoctrination, and to encourage self-transformation. We need to allow teacher candidates personal space for self-discovery.

Can one semester have any long-term influence on teacher dispositions? We are confident that some of our teacher candidates were positively affected by their intense, albeit limited, work with dispositions. During a recent program meeting, several adjunct university supervisors indicated that the quality level of recent teacher candidates was significantly improved. One adjunct excitedly shared, "This batch we have right now is absolutely incredible!" Another adjunct noted, "Teacher candidates want to talk about the good and the bad. . . . They are not a bit afraid of reflection." Still another chimed in, "I've never seen teacher candidates seek out information to this degree." These comments suggest truly collegial conversations, which provide evidence of reflection and continuous learning in action.

Adjuncts also mentioned a change in the type of confidence displayed by teacher candidates. In the past, it was more like "I know everything I need to know," which personified an in-your-face defensive attitude. Now teacher candidates' confidence is less egocentric and more professional—yet another disposition. They are confident that their knowledge and perspectives have value, but they manifest a higher level of respect for both their cooperating teacher and adjunct university supervisor.

Holistically, teacher candidates seem more actively engaged in the teaching and learning context. One adjunct talked about the "drama of the classroom—it just seems like the classroom environment is so much more alive. It seems to come from the fact that these teacher candidates really know who they are. They are really taking risks in the classroom—spontaneous role playing." While we cannot make a direct cause-and-effect connection, we do believe that as teacher candidates become more assured of their teacher identities they become more secure in their professional encounters.

We believe that when our teacher candidates systematically and intentionally look at teacher dispositions in the university and K–12 contexts, it promotes recognition of their value. But here again, this is just one semester at the end of the program. Where and when do you address dispositions in a teacher education program? Why and to what end? What influence do individual faculty members have over the content and delivery of dispositions within their program and how willing are they to live with these constraints? For secondary education programs, required courses are often taught outside of the education department. The logistics of this arrangement forces a new realm of collegiality among faculty.

The aforementioned conversation with our adjunct university supervisors, while illuminating and encouraging, adds another layer to the sphere of influence within a teacher education program. As we wrote this book and thought about our work with teacher dispositions, we inadvertently forgot to consider the role of non-faculty members. How do we help people in adjunct positions become vested in a teacher education program's work with dispositions?

The teaching profession requires us to frequently self-assess our work as planners, implementers, and administrators of teaching and learning within our classroom contexts. Do we give our teacher candidates sufficient training in this area so that they can determine the

questions to ask, how to evaluate the answers for validity, and ultimately, how to make the necessary adjustments to raise the quality
of the learning experiences in their K–12 classrooms?

> What bothers me is that when I was sitting in the classroom and you
> were teaching us all this stuff, it meant something to me then, but it
> means something different to me out here because I have to use it and
> it bothers me that I didn't think right away what to do. I must not have
> thought I was actually going to use this. And now I have to and I'm
> getting caught in this panic. It makes me wonder how many other
> things we're learning in our university classes that we don't pay the
> right attention to. We do the right thing as a student, but we don't do
> the right thing as far as giving it a place where it can be pulled up
> again when we get into the classroom. (TC 7)

Teachers at any stage of development can get caught up in moments
like those described above. We tell our teacher candidates that they
are crossing the threshold from student-learner to teacher-learner. It
is easy to forget that the threshold feels more like a chasm for some
of them. They are bombarded with newness that requires an agility
of thought and action to which they are not accustomed. This combined with a tenuous teacher identity fuels their anxiety, causing
them to seemingly forget everything they thought they knew.

Teacher candidates are also concerned about what to do if future
colleagues display less than positive teacher dispositions. They do
not want to become angry with or judgmental of these peers. Our
teacher candidates seem willing and able to monitor their own dispositions throughout their careers; but how will this change in their
first, second, and third years of teaching and beyond? Might there be
some connection to dispositions and the urban lore surrounding the
five-year attrition rate of new teachers?

Induction programs could provide teacher candidates with the structure to dig into their dispositions as they deal with new contexts—
confront new classroom challenges. We believe that teacher dispositions are as essential to the teaching and learning environment as

knowledge and skills. Therefore, we recommend that they be given equal emphasis when districts select professional development programs.

BON VOYAGE

Teacher dispositions are self-perpetuating; therefore, work with them should never feel "done." New experiences, contexts, and knowledge will push, pull, and prod us through the dynamics of interpersonal relationships and intrapersonal reflections with future generations of teacher candidates. Writing this book was a critical piece of our systematic and intentional examination of teacher dispositions. Our future journeys will need to include a similar process, but we do not know exactly what form it will take. Our intent in sharing our experiences is to spark conversation as you consider ways to adopt, adapt, or possibly disregard elements from our journey. If we succeeded, we wish you luck on your excursion and look forward to hearing about what *you* see!

Appendix One

Original Teacher Dispositions Rubric

Interactions with Others	A	B	C	D
Active engagement in small- or large-group settings	Consistently initiates thought-provoking discussions and responds to others' insights in ways that further the conversation and invoke new ways of thinking	Usually initiates thought-provoking discussions and responds to others' insights in ways that further the conversation and invoke new ways of thinking	Occasionally initiates thought-provoking discussions and responds to others' insights in ways that further the conversation and invoke new ways of thinking	Rarely if ever initiates thought-provoking discussions or responds to others' insights in ways that further the conversation or invoke new ways of thinking
Thoughtful and responsive listener	Clearly demonstrates the ability to listen to people's insights, needs, and concerns, then responds both positively and thoughtfully, e.g., asking a question or summarizing points	Usually demonstrates the ability to listen to people's insights, needs, and concerns, then responds both positively and thoughtfully, e.g., asking a question or summarizing points	Occasionally demonstrates the ability to listen to people's insights, needs, and concerns, then responds both positively and thoughtfully, e.g., asking a question or summarizing points	Rarely if ever demonstrates the ability to listen to people's insights, needs, and concerns and appears unable to respond either positively or thoughtfully
Cooperative and collaborative	Consistently works to keep the group on task, maximize individual talents, evenly distribute responsibility, etc.	Usually works to keep the group on task, maximize individual talents, evenly distribute responsibility, etc.	Occasionally works to keep the group on task, maximize individual talents, evenly distribute responsibility, etc.	Rarely if ever works to keep the group on task, maximize individual talents, evenly distribute responsibility, etc.

Respect for self and others	Consistently displays respect for others	Usually displays respect for others	Occasionally displays respect for others	Rarely if ever displays respect for others
Professionalism	A	B	C	D
Active engagement in reflection	Consistently willing to suspend initial judgments, be receptive of a critical examination of multiple perspectives, generate effective and productive options, make reasoned decisions with supporting evidence, and make connections to previous readings, experiences, courses, etc.	Usually willing to suspend initial judgments, be receptive of a critical examination of multiple perspectives, generate effective and productive options, make reasoned decisions with supporting evidence, and make connections to previous readings, experiences, courses, etc.	Occasionally willing to suspend initial judgments, be receptive of a critical examination of multiple perspectives, generate effective and productive options, make reasoned decisions with supporting evidence, and make connections to previous readings, experiences, courses, etc.	Rarely if ever willing to suspend initial judgments, be receptive of a critical examination of multiple perspectives, generate effective and productive options, make reasoned decisions with supporting evidence, and make connections to previous readings, experiences, courses, etc.
Preparedness	Consistently well prepared for class, e.g., completes reading assignments and is engaged in reading materials: written notes, questions, other responsibilities	Usually well prepared for class, e.g., completes reading assignments and is engaged in reading materials: written notes, questions, other responsibilities	Occasionally well prepared for class, e.g., completes reading assignments and is engaged in reading materials: written notes, questions, other responsibilities	Rarely if ever well prepared for class, e.g., completes reading assignments and is engaged in reading materials: written notes, questions, other responsibilities

(continued)

Professionalism	A	B	C	D
Involved in continuous learning	Consistently demonstrates curiosity, creativity, and flexibility regarding course content, processes, and tasks	Usually demonstrates curiosity, creativity, and flexibility regarding course content, processes, and tasks	Occasionally demonstrates curiosity, creativity, and flexibility regarding course content, processes, and tasks	Rarely if ever demonstrates curiosity, creativity, and flexibility regarding course content, processes, and tasks
Response to situations	Consistently responds competently and maturely to situations	Usually responds competently and maturely to situations	Occasionally responds competently and maturely to situations	Rarely if ever responds competently and maturely to situations
Response to feedback	Consistently responds professionally to feedback and suggestions and makes appropriate adjustments	Usually responds professionally to feedback and suggestions and makes appropriate adjustments	Occasionally responds professionally to feedback and suggestions and makes appropriate adjustments	Rarely if ever responds professionally to feedback and suggestions or makes appropriate adjustments
Attendance	Timely and consistently present in class	Few tardies or early departures OR 2 absences	Several tardies or early departures OR 3 absences	Numerous tardies and early departures OR 4+ absences

Appendix Two

Second Teacher Dispositions Rubric

	A	B	C	D
Large-group participation	Consistently engages in large-group setting, e.g., volunteers information and insights, asks questions of and responds to peers, contributes when called on, etc.	Usually engages in large-group setting, e.g., volunteers information and insights, asks questions of and responds to peers, contributes when called on, etc.	Occasionally engages in large group setting, e.g., volunteers information and insights, asks questions of and responds to peers, contributes when called on, etc.	Rarely if ever engages in large-group setting, e.g., volunteers information and insights, asks questions of and responds to peers, contributes when called on, etc.
Small-group participation	Consistently engages in small-group settings, e.g., initiates thought-provoking discussions, responds to others' insights in ways that further the conversation, invokes new ways of thinking, etc.	Usually engages in small-group settings, e.g., initiates thought-provoking discussions, responds to others' insights in ways that further the conversation, invokes new ways of thinking, etc.	Occasionally engages in small-group settings, e.g., initiates thought-provoking discussions, responds to others' insights in ways that further the conversation, invokes new ways of thinking, etc.	Rarely if ever engages in small-group settings, e.g., initiates thought-provoking discussions, responds to others' insights in ways that further the conversation, invokes new ways of thinking, etc.
Listening	Clearly demonstrates the ability to thoughtfully listen and respond to people's insights, needs, and concerns, e.g., asking a question, summarizing points, etc.	Usually demonstrates the ability to thoughtfully listen and respond to people's insights, needs, and concerns, e.g., asking a question, summarizing points, etc.	Occasionally demonstrates the ability to thoughtfully listen and respond to people's insights, needs, and concerns, e.g., asking a question, summarizing points, etc.	Rarely if ever demonstrates the ability to thoughtfully listen and respond to people's insights, needs, and concerns, e.g., asking a question, summarizing points, etc.

Cooperation and collaboration	Consistently works well with others, e.g., keeps the group on task, maximizes individuals' talents, evenly distributes responsibility, etc.	Usually works well with others, e.g., keeps the group on task, maximizes individuals' talents, evenly distributes responsibility, etc.	Occasionally works well with others, e.g., keeps the group on task, maximizes individuals' talents, evenly distributes responsibility, etc.	Rarely if ever works well with others, e.g., keeps the group on task, maximizes individuals' talents, evenly distributes responsibility, etc.
Respect	Consistently shows respect for self and others, e.g., interacts without putdowns or sarcasm, is sensitive to language use, sets high expectations, shows due courtesy and consideration for people and ideas, etc.	Usually shows respect for self and others, e.g., interacts without putdowns or sarcasm, is sensitive to language use, sets high expectations, shows due courtesy and consideration for people and ideas, etc.	Occasionally shows respect for self and others, e.g., interacts without putdowns or sarcasm, is sensitive to language use, sets high expectations, shows due courtesy and consideration for people and ideas, etc.	Rarely if ever shows respect for self and others, e.g., interacts without putdowns or sarcasm, is sensitive to language use, sets high expectations, shows due courtesy and consideration for people and ideas, etc.
Reflection	Consistently willing to suspend initial judgments, be receptive of a critical examination of multiple perspectives, generate effective and productive options, make reasoned decisions with supporting evidence, and make connections to previous readings, experiences, courses, etc.	Usually willing to suspend initial judgments, be receptive of a critical examination of multiple perspectives, generate effective and productive options, make reasoned decisions with supporting evidence, and make connections to previous readings, experiences, courses, etc.	Occasionally willing to suspend initial judgments, be receptive of a critical examination of multiple perspectives, generate effective and productive options, make reasoned decisions with supporting evidence, and make connections to previous readings, experiences, courses, etc.	Rarely if ever willing to suspend initial judgments, be receptive of a critical examination of multiple perspectives, generate effective and productive options, make reasoned decisions with supporting evidence, and make connections to previous readings, experiences, courses, etc.

(continued)

	A	B	C	D
Preparedness	Consistently well prepared for class, e.g., completes reading assignments and is engaged in reading materials: written notes, questions, other responsibilities	Usually well prepared for class, e.g., completes reading assignments and is engaged in reading materials: written notes, questions, other responsibilities	Occasionally well prepared for class, e.g., completes reading assignments and is engaged in reading materials: written notes, questions, other responsibilities	Rarely if ever well prepared for class, e.g., completes reading assignments and is engaged in reading materials: written notes, questions, other responsibilities
Continuous learning	Consistently demonstrates curiosity, creativity, and flexibility regarding course content, processes, tasks, etc.	Usually demonstrates curiosity, creativity, and flexibility regarding course content, processes, tasks, etc.	Occasionally demonstrates curiosity, creativity, and flexibility regarding course content, processes, tasks, etc.	Rarely if ever demonstrates curiosity, creativity, and flexibility regarding course content, processes, tasks, etc.
Professionalism	Consistently views feedback and situations maturely, analyzes feedback and makes appropriate adjustments to enhance personal growth and learning, and analyzes comments and interactions to make appropriate adjustments that promote a positive learning environment	Usually views feedback and situations maturely, analyzes feedback and makes appropriate adjustments to enhance personal growth and learning, and analyzes comments and interactions to make appropriate adjustments that promote a positive learning environment	Occasionally views feedback and situations maturely, analyzes feedback and makes appropriate adjustments to enhance personal growth and learning, and analyzes comments and interactions to make appropriate adjustments that promote a positive learning environment	Rarely if ever views feedback and situations maturely, analyzes feedback and makes appropriate adjustments to enhance personal growth and learning, and analyzes comments and interactions to make appropriate adjustments that promote a positive learning environment
Attendance	Timely and consistently present in class	Few tardies or early departures OR 2 absences	Several tardies or early departures OR 3 absences	Numerous tardies or early departures OR 4+ absences

Appendix Three

Narrative Outline of Teacher Dispositions

Promoting dispositions requisite of those in the teaching profession is increasingly being recognized as a fundamental responsibility of teacher education (please refer to the NCATE and INTASC websites linked to the SCSU College of Education homepage). To this end, we (Dr. Jenkins and I) compiled the characteristics listed below as an assessment tool. (There are also blank lines for you to add your own characteristics.) Over the course of the semester, we will monitor your attitudes and behaviors as displayed in class. We are including a form for you to monitor yourself as well. Then, we will each use this information to determine your dispositions at midterm and again at the end of the semester. You will receive a separate *Dispositions of teaching* score for each course. Please remember, other's perceptions do not always align with our own intentions; this assessment process is designed to bring the two together as often as possible.

Large-Group Participation

You actively engage in large-group settings, for example:

- Volunteering information and insights
- Asking questions of and responding to peers
- Contributing when called upon
-
-

Small-Group Participation

You actively engage in small-group settings, for example:

- Initiating thought-provoking discussions
- Responding to others' insights in ways that further the conversation
- Promoting new ways of thinking about educational situations
-
-

Listening

You thoughtfully listen and respond to people's insights, needs, and concerns, for example:

- Asking questions
- Summarizing ideas and concepts
-
-

Cooperation and Collaboration

You work well with others, for example:

- Keeping groups on task
- Maximizing individuals' talents
- Distributing responsibilities evenly
-
-

Respect

You show respect for self and others, for example:

- Interacting without putdowns and sarcasm
- Demonstrating sensitivity with respect to language use

- Setting high expectations regarding social interactions, cooperation, collaboration, etc.
- Showing due courtesy and consideration for people and ideas
-
-

Reflection

You engage in active reflection, for example:

- Willing to suspend initial judgment
- Demonstrating receptivity for the critical examination of multiple perspectives
- Making reasoned decisions with supporting evidence
- Generating effective and productive options to situations
- Making connections to previous readings, experiences, courses, etc.
-
-

Preparedness

You are prepared for class, for example:

- Displaying evidence of completed reading assignments
- Providing evidence of engagement with reading materials
-
-

Continuous Learning

You view education as a lifelong learning process, for example:

- Exhibiting curiosity about new and seemingly old concepts
- Displaying creative ideas about and applications to educational concepts

- Modeling flexibility regarding course content, process, and tasks
-
-

Professionalism

You respond professionally to situations and feedback, for example:

- Reacting maturely (every complaint is accompanied by possible solutions)
- Analyzing feedback and making appropriate adjustments to enhance personal growth and learning
- Analyzing situations, comments, and interactions and making appropriate adjustments to promote a positive learning environment
-
-

Attendance

- You are present in and on time to class.
-

Appendix Four

Self-Assessment of Teacher Dispositions

Directions: At the end of each class period, take some time to think about your dispositions as described in this packet. Decide whether you were exemplary (+), adequate (√), or a wee bit weak (–) in each area and mark each accordingly. Be sure to provide evidence/comments to support your self-evaluation.

DATE:	DATE:	DATE:	DATE:	DATE:	DATE:	DATE:	DATE:	DATE:	DATE:	DATE:	DATE:	DATE:	
													Large-group participation
													Small-group participation
													Thoughtful and responsive listener
													Cooperative and collaborative
													Respect
													Reflection
													Preparedness
													Continuous learning
													Professionalism
													Attendance
													Evidence and comments for the day

Appendix Five

Class Participation Rubric

	A	B	C	D
Preparedness	Consistently well prepared for class, e.g., completes reading assignments and is engaged in reading materials: written notes, questions, other responsibilities	Usually well prepared for class, e.g., completes reading assignments and is engaged in reading materials: written notes, questions, other responsibilities	Occasionally well prepared for class, e.g., completes reading assignments and is engaged in reading materials: written notes, questions, other responsibilities	Rarely if ever well prepared for class, e.g., completes reading assignments and is engaged in reading materials: written notes, questions, other responsibilities
Class contributions in large-group setting	Consistently engages in large-group setting, e.g., volunteers information and insights, asks questions of and responds to peers, and contributes when called on	Usually volunteers information and insights, asks questions of and responds to peers, and demonstrates willingness and ability to contribute when called on	Occasionally volunteers information and insights, asks questions of and responds to peers, and demonstrates willingness and ability to contribute when called on	Rarely if ever volunteers information and insights, asks questions of and responds to peers, or demonstrates willingness and ability to contribute when called on
Class contributions in small-group settings	Consistently engages in small-group settings, e.g., initiates thought-provoking discussions and responds to others' insights in ways that further the conversation and invoke new ways of thinking	Usually initiates thought-provoking discussions and responds to others' insights in ways that further the conversation and invoke new ways of thinking	Occasionally initiates thought-provoking discussions or responds to others' insights in ways that further the conversation and invoke new ways of thinking	Rarely if ever initiates thought-provoking discussions or responds to others' insights in ways that further the conversation or invoke new ways of thinking
Attendance	Timely and consistently present in class	Few tardies or early departures **OR 2** absences	Several tardies or early departures **OR 3** absences	Numerous tardies or early departures **OR 4+** absences

Appendix Six

Personal Qualitative Inventory of Dispositions

Note to readers: The information in this appendix is given to teacher candidates as a packet. The initial pages (which are reproduced here) contain the purpose and guidelines. Teacher candidates can then use the subsequent six pages, which are blank except for a disposition header, to record their respective evidence.

PURPOSE

Promoting dispositions requisite of those in the teaching profession is increasingly being recognized as a fundamental responsibility of teacher education (please refer to the NCATE and INTASC websites linked to the SCSU College of Education homepage). To this end, we (Dr. Jenkins and I) compiled the characteristics listed below as an assessment tool. Over the course of the semester, you will monitor your attitudes and behaviors regarding these six distinct dispositions as they are displayed in class, keeping a personal qualitative inventory (PQI).

DISPOSITIONS

Over the course of the semester, you will be working to develop and/or enhance the dispositions listed here (with room to add your own). You

should also keep a daily running record of the evidence of your attitudes and behaviors in each area. Please note that "evidence" is the
recording of specific details demonstrating personal actions and behaviors that are examples of the disposition rather than the recording of
what happened in class on a particular day. Periodically, you will share
your running record with me and/or your peers . . . the intent here is to
double-check that we are being perceived as we intended.

Continuous Learning

You view education as a lifelong learning process, for example:

- Exhibiting curiosity about new and seemingly old concepts
- Displaying creative ideas about and applications to educational
  concepts
- Modeling flexibility regarding course content, process, and tasks
-
-

Cooperation and Collaboration

You work well with others, for example:

- Keeping groups on task
- Maximizing individuals' talents
- Distributing responsibilities evenly
-
-

Listening

You thoughtfully listen and respond to people's insights, needs, and
concerns, for example:

- Asking questions
- Summarizing ideas and concepts
-
-

Respect

You show respect for self and others, for example:

- Interacting without putdowns and sarcasm
- Demonstrating sensitivity with respect to language use
- Setting high expectations regarding social interactions, cooperation, collaboration, etc.
- Showing due courtesy and consideration for people and ideas
-
-

Reflection

You engage in active reflection, for example:

- Monitoring and critiquing your attitudes and behaviors
- Willing to suspend initial judgments
- Demonstrating receptivity for the critical examination of multiple perspectives
- Making reasoned decisions with supporting evidence
- Generating effective and productive options to situations
- Making connections to previous readings, experiences, courses, etc.
-
-

Professionalism

You respond professionally to situations and feedback, for example:

- Reacting maturely (every complaint is accompanied by possible solutions)
- Analyzing feedback and making appropriate adjustments to enhance personal growth and learning
- Analyzing situations, comments, and interactions and making appropriate adjustments to promote a positive learning environment
-
-

Appendix Seven

Survey of Cooperating Teachers

The National Council for the Accreditation of Teacher Educators (NCATE, The Standard of Excellence in Teacher Preparation, 2000; www.ncate.org) asks teacher education programs to assess teacher dispositions. In turn, they define them as referring to the values, commitments, and professional ethics that influence behaviors toward students, families, colleagues, and communities and affect student learning, motivation, and development as well as the educator's own professional growth. Please read the 24 statements below and determine whether you AGREE, AGREE IN PART, HAVE NO OPINION, DISAGREE IN PART, or DISAGREE with each. **Circle** the appropriate response to each statement. Feel free to **add narrative comments** at any point on this survey.

Teachers should . . .

1. be committed to critical reflection for professional growth.

AGREE—AGREE IN PART—NO OPINION—
DISAGREE IN PART—DISAGREE

Comments: _____

_____

2. cooperate with colleagues in planning instruction.

AGREE—AGREE IN PART—NO OPINION—
DISAGREE IN PART—DISAGREE

Comments: _____

_____

3. actively seek out professional growth opportunities.

AGREE—AGREE IN PART—NO OPINION—
DISAGREE IN PART—DISAGREE

Comments: _____

_____

4. be thoughtful and responsive listeners.

AGREE—AGREE IN PART—NO OPINION—
DISAGREE IN PART—DISAGREE

Comments: _____

_____

5. demonstrate and encourage democratic interaction in the classroom and school.

AGREE—AGREE IN PART—NO OPINION—
DISAGREE IN PART—DISAGREE

Comments: _____

_____

6. engage in discussions about new ideas in the teaching profession.

AGREE—AGREE IN PART—NO OPINION—
DISAGREE IN PART—DISAGREE

Comments: _____

_____

7. engage in research-based teaching practices.

AGREE—AGREE IN PART—NO OPINION—
DISAGREE IN PART—DISAGREE

Comments: _____

_____

8. create connections to subject matter that are meaningful or relevant to students.

AGREE—AGREE IN PART—NO OPINION—
DISAGREE IN PART—DISAGREE

Comments: _____

_____

9. listen to colleagues' ideas and suggestions to improve instruction.

AGREE—AGREE IN PART—NO OPINION—
DISAGREE IN PART—DISAGREE

Comments: _____

_____

10. communicate effectively with students, parents, and colleagues.

AGREE—AGREE IN PART—NO OPINION—
DISAGREE IN PART—DISAGREE

Comments: _____

_____

11. work well with others in implementing a common curriculum.

AGREE—AGREE IN PART—NO OPINION—
DISAGREE IN PART—DISAGREE

Comments: _____

_____

12. use a variety of instructional strategies to optimize student learning.

AGREE—AGREE IN PART—NO OPINION—
DISAGREE IN PART—DISAGREE

Comments: _____

_____

13. stay current with the evolving nature of the teaching profession.

AGREE—AGREE IN PART—NO OPINION—
DISAGREE IN PART—DISAGREE

Comments: _____

_____

14. assume responsibility when working with others.

AGREE—AGREE IN PART—NO OPINION—
DISAGREE IN PART—DISAGREE

Comments: _____

_____

15. have high expectations for all students and help them achieve these.

AGREE—AGREE IN PART—NO OPINION—
DISAGREE IN PART—DISAGREE

Comments: _____

_____

16. view teaching as a collaborative effort among educators.

AGREE—AGREE IN PART—NO OPINION—
DISAGREE IN PART—DISAGREE

Comments: _____

_____

17. understand students have certain needs that must be met before learning can take place.

AGREE—AGREE IN PART—NO OPINION—
DISAGREE IN PART—DISAGREE

Comments: _____

_____

18. be sensitive to student differences.

AGREE—AGREE IN PART—NO OPINION—
DISAGREE IN PART—DISAGREE

Comments: _____

_____

19. treat students with dignity and respect at all times.

AGREE—AGREE IN PART—NO OPINION—
DISAGREE IN PART—DISAGREE

Comments: _____

_____

20. be willing to receive feedback and assessment of their teaching.

AGREE—AGREE IN PART—NO OPINION—
DISAGREE IN PART—DISAGREE

Comments: _____

_____

21. be patient when working with students.

AGREE—AGREE IN PART—NO OPINION—
DISAGREE IN PART—DISAGREE

Comments: _____

_____

22. be open to adjusting and revising plans to meet student needs.

AGREE—AGREE IN PART—NO OPINION—
DISAGREE IN PART—DISAGREE

Comments: _____

_____

23. communicate in ways that demonstrate respect for feelings, ideas, and contributions of others.

AGREE—AGREE IN PART—NO OPINION—
DISAGREE IN PART—DISAGREE

Comments: _____

_____

24. seriously consider the quality of their responses and reactions to situations and feedback from students, colleagues, parents, etc.

AGREE—AGREE IN PART—NO OPINION—
DISAGREE IN PART—DISAGREE

Comments: _____

_____

This survey was adapted from Schulte, L. E., Edick, N., Edwards, S., & Mackiel, D., "The Development and Validation of the Teacher Dispositions Index," paper presented at the annual meeting of the American Association of Teacher Educators, Chicago, February 2004.

Appendix Eight

Teacher Dispositions from PQI with Corresponding Survey Items

Teacher Disposition	Survey Items (Teachers Should . . .)
Continuous learning	3. actively seek out professional growth opportunities 6. engage in discussions about new ideas in the teaching profession 7. engage in research-based teaching practices 13. stay current with the evolving nature of the teaching profession
Cooperation and collaboration	2. cooperate with colleagues in planning instruction 5. demonstrate and encourage democratic interaction in the classroom and school 11. work well with others in implementing a common curriculum 14. assume responsibility when working with others
Listening	4. be thoughtful and responsive listeners 9. listen to colleagues' ideas and suggestions to improve instruction 10. communicate effectively with students, parents, and colleagues
Respect	15. have high expectations for all students and help them achieve their potential 19. treat students with dignity and respect at all times 21. be patient when working with students 23. communicate in ways that demonstrate respect for feelings, ideas, and contributions of others

(continued)

Teacher Disposition	Survey Items (Teachers Should . . .)
Reflection	1. be committed to critical reflection for professional growth 8. create connections to subject matter that are meaningful and relevant to students 12. use a variety of instructional strategies to optimize student learning 17. understand that students have certain needs that must be met before learning can take place 22. be open to adjusting and revising plans to meet student needs
Professionalism	16. view teaching as a collaborative effort among educators 18. be sensitive to student differences 20. be willing to receive feedback and assessment of their teaching 24. seriously consider the quality of their responses and reactions to situations and feedback from students, colleagues, parents, etc.

References

Albee, J. J., & Piveral, J. A. (2003). Management process for defining and monitoring teacher dispositions. *The International Journal of Educational Management, 17*(7), 346–356.

Balzano, B. A., & Murray, C. E. (2003, January). *Do you know them when you see them? Teacher candidate dispositions.* Paper presented at the annual meeting of the American Association of Colleges of Teacher Education, New Orleans.

Banner, J., Jr., & Cannon, H. (1997). *The elements of teaching.* New Haven: Yale University Press.

Brookfield, S. (1995). *Becoming a critically reflective teacher.* San Francisco, CA: Jossey-Bass.

Caine, R. N., & Caine, G. (1991). *Making connections: Teaching and the human brain.* Alexandria, VA: Association for Supervision and Curriculum Development.

Certo, J. L., & Fox, J. E. (2002). Retaining quality teachers. *High School Journal, 86*(1), 57–75.

Collinson, V. (1996). *Becoming an exemplary teacher: Integrating profession, interpersonal and intrapersonal knowledge.* (ERIC Document Reproduction Service No. ED410227)

Csikszentmihalyi, M. (1990). *Flow: The psychology of optimal experience.* New York: Harper and Row.

Damasio, A. R. (1994). *Descartes' error: Emotion, reason, and the human brain.* New York: Grosset/Putnam.

Danielewicz, J. (2001). *Teaching selves: Identity, pedagogy, and teacher education.* Albany, NY: State University of New York Press.

Darling-Hammond, L., & Sclan, E. M. (1996). Who teaches and why: Dilemmas of building a profession for twenty-first century schools. In J. Sikula, T. J. Buttery, & E. Guyton (Eds.), *Handbook of research on teacher education* (2nd ed., pp. 67–101). New York: Macmillan.

Deal, T. E., & Chatman, R. M. (1989). Learning the ropes alone: Socializing new teachers. *Action in Teacher Education, 11*(1), 21–29.

Demmon-Berger, D. (1986). *Effective teaching: Observations from research.* (ERIC Document Reproduction Service No. ED274087)

Dewey, J. (1933). *How we think: A restatement of the relation of reflective thinking to the educative process.* Lexington, MA: D.C. Heath.

Dewey, J. (1944). *Democracy and education.* New York: The Free Press.

Dinkelman, T. (2003). Self-study in teacher education: A means and ends tool for promoting reflective teaching. *Journal of Teacher Education, 54*(1), 6–18.

DuFour, R., & Eaker, R. (1998). *Professional learning communities at work: Best practices for enhancing student achievement.* Bloomington, IN: Solution Tree.

Educational Testing Services. Rosedale Road, Princeton, NJ. www.ets.org.

Engle, S. H., & Ochoa, A. S. (1988). *Education for democratic citizenship: Decision making in the social studies.* New York: Teachers College Press.

Fehn, B., & Koeppen, K. E. (1998). Intensive document-based instruction in a social studies methods course. *Theory and Research in Social Education, 26*(4), 461–484.

Feiman-Nemser, S. (2001). From preparation to practice: Designing a continuum to strengthen and sustain teaching. *Teacher's College Record, 103*, 1013–1055.

Good, T., & Brophy, J. (1994). *Looking in classrooms* (6th ed.). New York: HarperCollins.

Goodlad, J. (1990). *Teachers for our nation's schools.* San Francisco: Jossey-Bass.

Goodlad, J. (1994). *Educational renewal.* San Francisco: Jossey-Bass.

Goodman, J. (1986). University education courses and the professional preparation of teachers: A descriptive analysis. *Teaching & Teacher Education, 2*(4), 341–353.

Goodman, J., & Fish, D. R. (1997). Against-the-grain teacher education: A study of coursework, field experience, and perspectives. *Journal of Teacher Education, 48*(2), 96–107.

Grossman, P. L. (1990). *The making of a teacher: Teacher knowledge and teacher education.* NY: Teachers College.

Holmes Group. (1995). *Tomorrow's schools of education.* East Lansing, MI: Author.

Interstate New Teacher Assessment and Support Consortium. (1992). *Model standards for beginning teacher licensing and development: A resource for state dialogue.* Washington, DC: Council of Chief State School Officers. Retrieved February 3, 2002, from www.ccsso.org/intasc.html.

Johnson, D., Johnson, R., & Holubec, E. (1998). *Cooperation in the classroom* (7th ed.). Edina, MN: Interaction Book Company.

Kauchak, D., & Eggen, P. (2003). *Learning and teaching: Research-based methods* (4th ed.). Boston, MA: Allyn & Bacon.

Kennedy, M. M. (1997). *Defining an ideal teacher education program* (mimeo). Washington, DC: National Council for the Accreditation of Teacher Education.

Koeppen, K. E. (1996). *The fabric of planning: Unraveling the complexities of secondary student teachers' instructional planning processes.* Unpublished doctoral dissertation, University of Iowa, Iowa City.

Koeppen, K. E., & Davison-Jenkins, J. (2006). Do you see what I see? Helping secondary preservice teachers recognize and monitor their teacher disposition. *Action in Teacher Education, 28*(1), 13–26.

Kottler, J., & Zehm, S. (2000). *On being a teacher.* Thousand Oaks, CA: Corwin.

LaBoskey, V. (1994). *Development of reflective practice.* New York: Teachers College Press.

Leithwood, K. (1990). The principal's role in teacher development. In B. Joyce (Ed.), *Changing school culture through staff development* (pp. 71–90). Washington, DC: Association for Supervision and Curriculum Development.

Levine, A. (2006). Educating School Teachers (Education Schools Project Report #2). Retrieved October 12, 2006, from www.edschools.org/teacher_report.htm.

Lortie, D. (1975). *Schoolteacher.* Chicago: University of Chicago Press.

Martinello, M., & Cook, G. (2000). *Interdisciplinary inquiry in teaching and learning* (2nd. ed.). Upper Saddle River, NJ: Prentice-Hall, Inc.

Maylone, N. (2002). *Identifying desirable pre-service teacher dispositions: An intractable problem?* (ERIC Document Reproduction Service No. ED463258)

Minnesota Board of Teaching. (2000). *Minnesota Standards of Effective Practice.* Retrieved August 25, 2001, from www.revisor.leg.state.mn.us/arule/8710/2000.html.

National Council for the Accreditation of Teacher Educators. (2000). *The standard of excellence in teacher preparation.* Retrieved January 12, 2002, from www.ncate.org.

Noddings, N. (1992). *The challenge to care in schools.* New York: Teachers College Press.

Noddings, N. (1995). Teaching themes of care. *Phi Delta Kappan, 76*(9), 675–679.

Palmer, P. (1998). *The courage to teach: Exploring the inner landscape of a teacher's life.* San Francisco: Jossey-Bass.

Parker, W. C. (2002). *Teaching democracy: Unity and diversity in public life.* New York: Teachers College Press.

Peterson, P. L., Wilkinson, L. C., & Hallinan, M. (1984). *The social context of instruction: Group organization and group processes.* San Diego, CA: Harcourt, Brace, Jovanovich.

Powers, S. M. (1999). *Transmission of teacher dispositions: A new use for electronic dialogue.* (ERIC Document Reproduction Service No. ED432307)

Raths, J. (2001). *Teachers' beliefs and teaching beliefs.* (ERIC Document Reproduction Service No. ED452999)

Roberts, P., & Kellough, R. (2000). *A guide for developing interdisciplinary thematic units* (2nd. ed.). Upper Saddle River, NJ: Prentice-Hall, Inc.

Rokeach, M. (1968). *Beliefs, attitudes, and values.* San Francisco: Jossey-Bass.

Ross, E. W. (1988). Becoming a teacher: The development of preservice teacher perspective. *Action in Teacher Education, 10*(2), 101–109.

Ruddell, R. B. (1995). Those influential literacy teachers: Meaning negotiators and motivation builders. *The Reading Teacher, 48*(6), 454–463.

Ryder, R., & Graves, M. (2003). *Reading and learning in content areas* (3rd ed.). New York: John Wiley & Sons.

Sarason, S. (1972). *The culture of the school and the problem of change* (2nd ed.). Newton, MA: Allyn & Bacon.

Schulte, L. E., Edick, N., Edwards, S., & Mackiel, D. (2004, February). *The development and validation of the teacher dispositions index*. Paper presented at the annual meeting of the American Association of Teacher Educators, Chicago.

Su, J. Z. X. (1992). Sources of influence in preservice teacher socialization. *Journal of Education for Teaching, 18*(3), 239–258.

Taylor, R. L., & Wasicsko, M. M. (2000, November). *The dispositions to teach*. Paper presented at the annual Southern Regional Association of Teacher Educators Conference, Lexington, KY.

Usher, D. (2002, November). *Arthur Combs' five dimensions of helper belief reformulated as five dispositions of teacher effectiveness*. Paper presented at the first annual Symposium on Educator Dispositions: Effective Teacher—Effective Person, Eastern Kentucky University.

Valli, L. (1992). *Reflective teacher education: Cases and critiques*. New York: SUNY.

Valli, L. (1997). Listening to other voices: A description of teacher reflection in the United States. *Peabody Journal of Education, 72*(1), 67–88.

Wenzlaff, T. L. (1998). Dispositions and portfolio development: Is there a connection? *Education, 118*(4), 564(9). Retrieved May 13, 2003, from infotrac.com.

Wood, K. (2005). *Interdisciplinary instruction: A practical guide for elementary and middle school teachers* (3rd. ed.). Upper Saddle River, NJ: Prentice-Hall, Inc.

Yost, D. S. (1997). The moral dimensions of teaching and preservice teachers: Can moral dispositions be influenced? *Journal of Teacher Education, 48*(4), 281–292.

About the Authors

Kim E. Koeppen is an associate professor in the Education Department of the College of Liberal Arts at Hamline University in St. Paul, Minnesota. She teaches courses in educational foundations, cultural diversity, and social studies methods and supervises secondary student teachers. Kim earned her doctorate in curriculum and instruction from the University of Iowa. Prior to that, she taught high school social studies near Chicago. Her scholarly interests include the teacher socialization process and social studies education; her leisure pursuits include biking and reading mysteries.

Judith Davison-Jenkins is an associate professor in the Teacher Development Department at St. Cloud State University in St. Cloud, Minnesota. She supervises student teachers and teaches courses addressing the needs of English language learners in K–12 classrooms and general methods with a literacy emphasis. Judy enjoyed teaching various literacy courses in grades 6–12 for over three decades before her present experience in higher education. She earned her doctorate in teaching and learning from the University of North Dakota. In her spare time she reads, gardens, and looks for new adventures.